Praise for *From Te...*

"Another stellar book by Sac... *Finding Your Way as a First-Time Leader without Losing ...* really resonated with me. Many thoughts and ideas were shared that would benefit any leader whether a veteran, beginner, or aspiring. This book allows the reader to reflect, learn, and grow as they build their personal leadership style. I personally appreciate the honesty and transparency that Starr shared. The importance of relationships and feedback are addressed throughout and truly are the foundation of effective leadership. I can't wait to share this with my mentors and fellow aspiring school leaders!"

—Jodie Pierpoint, aspiring leader

"Leaving the classroom for a leadership position is not always easy even after the decision has been made. In *From Teacher to Leader: Finding Your Way as a First-Time Leader without Losing Your Mind*, Starr Sackstein uses her usual raw honesty (which I happen to find refreshing) to help new leaders negotiate their way through the transition. This book is about more than our profession; it's about life."

—Peter DeWitt, EdD, author/consultant,
Education Week Finding Common Ground blog

"Our very best teachers are also leaders, and our very best leaders never stop teaching. *From Teacher to Leader* is written by Starr Sackstein, a person who has always been a master leader, albeit while serving as a classroom teacher. As Starr moved from the classroom into an official 'administrative' leadership role, she experienced many successes as well as challenges. This book captures her journey in a compelling way and will serve as an excellent resource for any educator moving from the classroom into an administrative role. The book is filled with sound advice, practical strategies, and inspiring stories. Each chapter includes helpful questions designed to help readers reflect on what they are doing, where they have been, and where they are going in their career. I highly recommend this well-written, important book."

—Jeffrey Zoul, EdD, author, speaker, leadership coach,
and president of ConnectEDD

"Sacktein's latest book on educational leadership in the twenty-first century is a shining star for the simple fact that it gives an honest look at what it takes to not only land your first job as a school- or district-based leader but actually be successful. This important book places a strong emphasis on relationships, growth, and a commitment to doing what's best for kids all day, every day. New to the world of leadership? Buy this book today!"

—**Brad Currie**, 2017 NASSP National Assistant Principal of the Year

"This story of a remarkably gifted teacher's journey into administration after her first year is a great read. After sixteen years developing consummate teaching skills, Starr's reflections, research efforts, and writing skills have resulted in a valuable resource for teachers considering a jump to administration and for experienced administrators as well. She truly lives up to her desire of becoming the kind of leader she would want to have. As an educator since 1969 and an administrator for thirty years, I find her advice to be spot-on. Make sure you and your professional development library have a copy."

—**Dr. Doug Green**, educational consultant and blogger

"Starr and I go back a few years now, and I have lived through her growth via conversations and online discussions but mostly by reading her books along the way. I have seen her progress from her initial foray into education with *Teaching Mythology Exposed* and observed her growth in blogging, questioning homework and grading, and even questioning questioning.

"Starr is passionate about relevance in schools. She clearly demonstrated relevance in the classroom and is now seeking relevance as an administrator.

"Her latest book, *From Teacher to Leader*, chronicles that journey clearly and concisely. Starr, never afraid to take on a new challenge, is approaching this new role in her positive style. The book flows very well, beginning with a succinct portrait of Starr by her current superintendent, Dan Rehman, and addressing many important topics for someone considering leaving the classroom for an administrative position.

"Starr speaks to the differences in being a teacher as a leader and leading teachers as an administrator. Defining her experiences very well, Starr lays it out there so prospective administrators have a clear view and understanding of the challenges each may face.

"*From Teacher to Leader* is a must-read for anyone considering leaving the classroom for an administrative position. Her latest creation will find a place on my bookshelf along with Starr's other books, reminding me that we must be passionate, caring, and questioning as we move through our educational lives."

—**Dr. Michael Curran**, professor of teacher education at Rider University

"I have had the distinct pleasure of collaborating with and growing into the role of an administrator alongside Starr Sackstein. *From Teacher to Leader* is incredibly insightful, practical, and is written in a manner that provides someone entering the administrative realm with both practical strategies and 'big ideas' that could immediately inform practice and pedagogy. This book is a must-read for administrators who are beginning their journey as well as for those who want to continually reflect on best practice in their leadership roles."

—**Greg Fredricks**, assistant principal, LaGrange Middle School, New York

"Not since former NYS Commissioner of Education Thomas Sobol's *My Life in School* has there been such a powerful personal reflection by a leader about school leadership. Looking back over his career, Sobol revealed the effect of his struggles and successes. He shared how it *felt* to be a leader, not simply what happened. In complementary fashion, Starr Sackstein writes from where she presently stands and looks forward. Her experiences are those happening right now in an educational world we can all identify with because we are all living in that world. She describes the pull toward leadership as it sits in contrast with the hesitation to leave the classroom where comfort and success reside. Each of her steps and stages and struggles weave together to be an important story all can understand and learn from. Her story is happening now. Her compelling revelations serve as a shared journey that can help escort others to move from a classroom to a leadership team."

—Jill Berkowicz, educator and author

"If you follow the work of Starr Sackstein (and you should), you're aware that she is known for several books she has already written along with her popular *Education Week* column, Work in Progress, and her passion for teaching without grades. Recently Sackstein made the jump from classroom to administration, and she's decided to 'tell all' in her latest book, *From Teacher to Leader*, which documents her first year out of the classroom. This is the perfect book for teachers looking to make the jump into administration, as the author beautifully intertwines her stories with explicit tips from which any administrator (new or old) could benefit. As I read through the book, I couldn't help but wish it had been written before I became an administrator. I highly recommend this book. Much credit to Sackstein for putting herself out there in her first year on the job!"

—Ross Cooper, principal of T. Baldwin Demarest Elementary School,
author of Hacking Project Based Learning

"If you are a teacher contemplating whether or not administration is for you, this book is the resource you need to help you decide. In *From Teacher to Leader*, author Starr Sackstein has written a step-by-step guide for teachers who are looking for a potential career change. Sackstein strategically walks the reader through her own experiences, describing in honest and transparent detail the challenges she encountered. More importantly, she provides relevant tips from the field on how to overcome those challenges."

—Jimmy Casas, educator, author, speaker, leadership coach

From
Teacher
to
LEADER

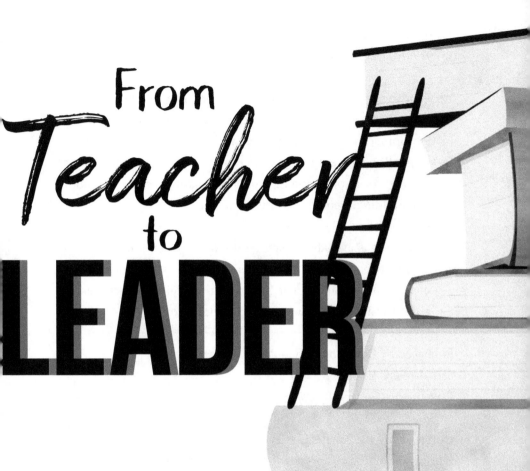

Finding Your Way
as a First-Time Leader
without Losing Your Mind

Starr Sackstein

From Teacher to Leader
© 2019 by Starr Sackstein

This book is available at special discounts when purchased in quantity for use as premiums, promotions, fundraisers, or for educational use. For inquiries and details, contact the publisher at books@daveburgessconsulting.com.

Published by Dave Burgess Consulting, Inc.
San Diego, CA
DaveBurgessConsulting.com

Cover Design by Genesis Kohler
Editing and Interior Design by My Writers' Connection

Library of Congress Control Number: 2019931162
Paperback ISBN: 978-1-949595-20-8
Ebook ISBN: 978-1-949595-21-5

First Printing: February 2019

Dedication

To all of the school leaders I have worked with over the years who taught me what to do—and what not to do. This would not have been possible without you.

To my husband, Charlie, who not only always reminds me to eat a good meal every day but also makes sure I actually eat it! You have supported me through tough times and constantly encourage me to do my best. Thank you for always reminding me if I can't do it now, it's just a matter of *yet*.

Contents

Foreword

My phone rang in mid-August. Ms. Sackstein was inquiring again as to the status of her potential employment in our school district. We'd had numerous exchanges throughout the summer attempting to determine whether she was eligible to become the director of Humanities at the beginning of the school year.

Let me rewind for a moment.

As I scrolled through numerous applications on a web-based service, I found many mistake-laden résumés and cover letters poorly tailored for the job; then, one résumé piqued my interest—and not just because the name *Starr Sackstein* tends to stand out. Her résumé was well written, and after reading it, her name stuck in my mind, though I could not match the résumé and name with my knowledge of Ms. Sackstein. When I asked our Kindergarten Center Principal, Faith Tripp, she immediately replied, "Twitter."

Starr has a presence on social media—particularly on Twitter, where she has quite a following. At that point, I was not one of them (sorry, Starr), but I had read retweets of her posts on occasion and, with her résumé on my screen, I clicked Follow. Ms. Sackstein was not chosen because of Twitter, however. If she had been, it would be an injustice to the body of work she has created thus far in her career. Starr was chosen to be the director of Humanities for her accomplishments, her willingness to be a risk taker, her high expectations for students and colleagues, and her intelligence.

Our interview process began with a screening interview, which typically lasts only fifteen to twenty minutes. Starr walked in dressed like someone who wanted the job. She had a firm handshake and made eye contact—qualities seemingly lost today—along with well-written cover letters and résumés, knowing how to code switch (speaking appropriately for an interview and not as if with friends on a Friday evening), and writing thank-you notes after an interview.

Starr's subsequent interview with the former superintendent and me was on-point and detailed. She was well able to answer the questions and provide insights into who she was as an educator. The only issue was that she was not certified as an administrator. We decided we would cross this bridge if the time arose.

After the few remaining candidates completed their interviews with a committee of administrators, teachers, and parents, the decision moved to the superintendent, who selected Starr to move on to meet the Board of Education. Led by Karen Brohm, our Board of Education is a dedicated group of seven community members who truly put first the good of all students. While I sensed some nervous energy emanating from Starr, she walked in, introduced herself to the Board, and commenced to tell them her understanding of students, school, and learning. Their only reservation was her having the appropriate certification, and I was able to explain alternative certifications were available in situations like this. Based on this, they agreed that the superintendent should offer Starr the position on the condition she met all the criteria for alternative certification.

Then the fun began.

I contacted Starr and worked with her to ensure all appropriate paperwork was completed and ready for presentation to the superintendent before she began her new role as director of Humanities. There were additional bumps along the way. Starr had to resign her current position even though the job with us was contingent upon meeting all the criteria, including passing two leadership exams, entering a certification program, and submitting a leadership portfolio to the state—all before starting her courses. Also, during this time, she had no health insurance for herself or her son. She was entrusting me—someone she had only met with for a total of two hours—with securing her future employment. Starr is definitely a risk taker!

Working with Starr seemed natural. She was a talented educator who had yet to fulfill her promise as a leader. I was also a *work in progress* (no, I am not stealing your blog name, Starr), who came into education from the banking world. We were both in education with a mission to lead our students down a more vibrant, engaging, and challenging learning path. We eventually exchanged our educational stories and beliefs—both of which aligned.

Starr and I spoke at least three times a week to report progress on what was completed, what was not, and what needed to be done next. Finding a college program during the summer was challenging—especially when we discovered we only had *one* option for alternative certification rather than several, as we'd previously thought. As it turned out, only one university offered the needed program, and of course, it was the one furthest away.

Our district submitted the needed paperwork, and Starr applied to the program and registered for courses. July became August, and the reality that we still did not have a director of Humanities was apparent. As I continued to give our superintendent updates, at several points in August we thought our plan was not going to come together in a timely fashion.

Then we hit a pothole.

Starr needed to take the state certification exam, but the early-summer exam deadline had passed. If she waited to take the next exam later in the summer, the results would not be available until late September. This would not work. The district was at a crossroad.

Fortunately, the superintendent reached out to someone she knew in the state education office who was able to process the paperwork for the earlier exam. With this hurdle cleared, Starr was now in a position to complete the requirements needed to be appointed as our new director.

Since Starr was not certified when the school year began and could not take on the typical roles and responsibilities of a director until she received her test score, she was assigned a mentor to learn alongside. Starr learned the lay of the land and how each building operated, started to place names with faces, and began to establish relationships. Eventually, her *passing* test score arrived, and Starr began her journey as the director of Humanities.

Throughout this interview and certification process, Starr embodied all the characteristics one would want in an educator and leader. She was enthusiastic, goal focused, persistent, self-aware, creative, innovative, willing to take risks, and reflective. She exhibited all of this without knowing me or anyone else in our organization.

Starr is a self-described *dork*; however, in my opinion, she is a passionate lifelong learner. She can establish goals based on relevant information and research, set deadlines, formulate plans, and implement them to reach her goals. Starr is reflective. She is particularly hard on herself (not a bad quality, in my opinion), readily admits to mistakes, and sets a course to correct them. Starr recently led some of our staff on curriculum-writing journeys, and the end products are both creative and forward thinking. I believe our students will greatly benefit from the words on the curriculum map coming to life.

Starr will likely find that leadership, like learning, is a never-ending journey. She will always find something to learn about the form or function of her school or the staff she is leading. But she is starting her leadership journey far ahead of many others—possessing qualities no one can remove, discount, or confuse.

Now if I can only convince her to drink Georgio's coffee without all the cancer-causing fake sugar!

Dan Rehman, superintendent
West Hempstead Union Free School District

Looking Back to Move Forward

Most (if not all) teachers have a *why* story that they add chapters to as the years and students touch their hearts. They make families within their schools and learning communities. As they continue to grow as educators, regardless of whether they stay in the classroom or go to another position, they must reimagine themselves in order to stay relevant and excited about the work they are doing.

At least that is my *why* story.

From the second I decided education was my path, I never allowed *good enough* to be part of my story. My journey as an educator has been a constant struggle between being memorable and pushing harder. With each turn, I had to make difficult decisions—whether I was considering a lateral move to a new school or district better aligned with my progress or looking at switching educational positions to keep growing.

Early in my career, I was great at developing relationships with students and consistently helping them understand they matter. I was also good at using any means necessary to create a classroom environment that students found engaging. While I wouldn't say I was necessarily a *great* teacher, I have worked hard to be better than good at these things.

By my third teaching position—six years into my education career—I thought I had found my forever home. I felt wanted and as if I was truly part of the school community. I took off my training wheels and stretched my legs. I honed my abilities as a risk taker and positive deviant and was committed to make learning possible for all. During my nine-year tenure in that position, I built a newspaper program defining my career and the path I would walk for a long time afterward. Journalism education became my obsession, and I grew so much from the help of those I befriended along the way and especially from my students.

During those years, however, I also struggled with boredom and dissatisfaction with administrative decisions. I took matters into my own hands when I didn't get the feedback I needed to keep growing, achieving National Board Certification, beginning my blog, and writing the books paving the path I had started to carve. The more connected I became, the better my pedagogy became and the brighter my students' outcomes shined.

Quietly, behind my closed classroom door, I began experimenting with grading less, and students began a flurry of reflection and problem solving. Together we questioned what learning should look like. During this time, colleagues and friends recommended I become an administrator. While I knew I had the skill set, my commitment was to the students with whom I was constantly growing.

Teacher leadership wasn't a stretch, though, and I became a mentor for new teachers. I sat on a multitude of committees in our small school, ranging from the professional development committee to the portfolio committee. I helped design curriculum, wrote assessment policies, and my classroom was used as a model space for teachers to visit. I welcomed each challenge.

Before long, I was ready for another chapter in my story, moving me closer to my current role. At a new school, I became an instructional coach while remaining a classroom teacher. This hybrid position gave me my first glimpse behind the administrative closed doors of cabinet meetings, data meetings, and instructional planning. Being responsible for the Teacher's Center (a resource space for teachers to collaborate, work, and learn with me or independently) while also teaching courses quickly established that I was up to the task of teaching students *and* helping colleagues grow their capacity for deeper student-centered learning. Whether I was visiting classrooms, sharing feedback, offering professional development, or working with teachers one-on-one, my job as an instructional coach showed me how much impact good leaders can have even if they aren't in the classroom all of the time.

Unfortunately, that year was a challenging one for me personally. In sixteen years as a teacher, I hadn't had a "doozy" like that one since my divorce almost a decade prior. My life circumstances and the physical location of the school created a perfect storm, pushing me to look for a new position closer to home. I found what I thought would be the ideal position, one I had always thought I could do—*if* I ever decided to try leadership.

The position called for an administrative license, and I didn't have one. But the job description was perfect, and I was certain the school could be my *new* forever home—if I could secure the position. Up to this point, life and what I perceived as the obstacles of a leadership position had kept me from taking the leap. This time something felt different. I applied for the job with high hopes but low expectations.

By the time I received a call about my application, so much time had passed I didn't even remember the specifics of the job. I was invited to do a twenty-minute screening interview, and even though I didn't know what that meant, I felt I had nothing to lose. I pulled my interview suit out of the closet, covered my tattoos, and went to my "speed date." The rest, as they say, is history.

From Teacher to Leader invites you into my first year as a leader— the good, the bad, and the learning. I hope that my experience and learning will help you find your own journey and decide if you are ready to take the leap out of the classroom. Throughout the book I have included excerpts from my *Education Week* teacher blog, *Work in Progress*, written during my transition from the classroom. These authentic moments offer a raw and uncensored look inside my feelings and the challenges I faced as a new leader as well as how those experiences impacted me and my decisions. I hope these reflective thoughts will help you explore your own journey and consider the multiple perspectives you may encounter from those you work with. At the end of each chapter, I have also included questions designed to encourage you to dig deeper into your current situation, consider your options, and help yourself grow.

CHAPTER 1

To Leave or Not to Leave?

> THE MOST DIFFICULT THING IS THE DECISION TO ACT, THE REST IS MERELY TENACITY. THE FEARS ARE PAPER TIGERS. YOU CAN DO ANYTHING YOU DECIDE TO DO. YOU CAN ACT TO CHANGE AND CONTROL YOUR LIFE; AND THE PROCEDURE, THE PROCESS IS ITS OWN REWARD.
>
> –Amelia Earhart

When do you know it is time to leave the classroom—this place you love and have found a home in—a place you've fallen in and out of love with and a place known to break your heart and rebuild it in a day? How do you know when it is time to leave a place that largely defines who you are?

The simple answer is, *you don't*. There is no single right way to know when to leave.

Much like starting a family, no matter how much you prepare or *think* you prepare, the right time doesn't magically show up just because you think it should. The ebbs and flows of life don't usually provide those momentous sea-separating experiences to show you the way. Defining moments are usually less obvious, and the key is knowing when to blindly jump into the abyss and brace for the coming impact.

Growing up, I never thought I'd be a teacher. But once I became one, I knew I could be nothing else. I was defined, in part, by being a high school English teacher. A good class, a small shared exchange with a student, or a *thank you* could turn a bad day into a good one, and as I grew more expert in my craft, I could confidently say I wish I'd had a teacher like me when I was growing up. (Over the years, I have amassed a drawer full of thank-you notes from parents *and* students to support my confidence.)

Despite my love of the classroom, I felt uneasy staying in the same position. I have a tendency to bore easily, and I knew that if I wasn't growing, I was going backward—and that was *not* an option. I had considered changing positions, but I only vaguely thought about leaving the classroom; in fact, I specifically chose not to get my administrative license because I didn't want to have the option. I opted instead for National Board Certification to further my education and pushed myself harder by digging deeper into my craft.

I knew that if I wasn't growing, I was going backward— and that was not an option.

Foundational Shifts

During the sixteen years I taught high school English, my belief system, practice, and philosophy evolved, propelling me in different directions at times—in terms of both of my practices and the roles I took on—despite my deep commitment to student learning. These tides of change in experiences colored how and what I thought in the classroom, and my perception adjusted accordingly, though I realized later that these shifts had to happen gradually if they were to be authentic and lasting.

The longer I spent in the classroom exposed to different ideas, the more I shifted and started taking more risks. It is with both pride and shame that I admit the teacher I was when I left the classroom was barely recognizable to the one who had entered it in her early twenties. In my early career, I was deeply entrenched in dogma from my own learning experiences and, therefore, didn't do enough to help all learners. Unfortunately, I was too ignorant and naive to see how my practice limited my students' growth. But I was willing to learn from anyone and eager to truly listen to students, and as a result, the way I taught and thought improved and expanded.

Watch for the Signs

Teachers consider leaving the classroom for a variety of reasons. For some teachers, the first time they consider moving into leadership is when an administrator or colleague asks them to think about a change. Others, as I did, exhibit some of the signs as shown on the following page and feel prompted to make a move.

SIGN: BOREDOM

MEANING: You still love the kids, but you are bored with the lessons you are teaching and the routine of daily responsibilities you once found exciting. While this could lead to more risk taking and research if you felt it could improve your job experience, it could mean it is time to try a new challenge.

SIGN: RESTLESSNESS

MEANING: You start looking at other professions—not just other jobs. You start thinking about how much of your life you've given to your current job and what you have gotten out of it. You're reflective, but not necessarily in a productive way. You have energy needing to be redirected, possibly the impetus to try something new. You must be bold if you stay where you are, or restlessness can lead to poor decision making.

SIGN: IRRITABILITY

MEANING: You are bothered—perhaps irrationally—by things previously not troubling. You're easily upset, and your level of satisfaction from your work is consistently poor. You still love the kids, but feel their behaviors are a personal affront. You also think you can do other people's jobs better than they can. When your patience starts to wane, look deeper into why.

SIGN: COMPLACENCY

MEANING: You start to *phone it in*. Things come easily to you, and you feel no need or desire to push harder because of other things happening in your life. You acknowledge this isn't the best version of yourself when you notice; you may even be nostalgic for previous times when you were great at your job;

in fact, you want to return to the best version of yourself. Are you feeling burned out, and is that why you aren't trying as hard? Only you can figure out if pushing through this difficult time is what's best or if a new challenge will reinvigorate your interest in this career.

SIGN: WILLINGNESS TO TAKE RISKS

MEANING: You take more calculated risks. You try new things and get more involved in professional learning outside of work. You readily apply what you learn because you want to be great at your job and don't have the fears new educators have. You have experience and a toolbox, and you're hungry for more.

SIGN: CONSTANT QUESTIONING OF PURPOSE IN YOUR CURRENT POSITION

MEANING: Because you've excelled in the classroom for a long time, you start to think you could share your experience and knowledge with a team. You consider your purpose and ask if your current position is the best fit for you. You seek answers in different places, connecting online with other educators, going back to school, or exploring options to stay fresh.

SIGN: DIRECT SUGGESTION

MEANING: An administrator or colleague asks you directly to consider a change. They have noticed your leadership abilities and encourage you to share those beyond the classroom.

If you notice any of these signs in your life, perhaps you need to think about switching your role.

Responding to the Signs

If you recognize any of these signs in yourself, or someone has suggested you consider a shift in your current position because you've shown leadership abilities, you need to take necessary action. Even if you don't switch positions or schools immediately, you should thoroughly consider a possible change. Any of the following may help you make an informed decision:

Search within your district or at local universities for leadership programs to identify what classes you'd need to take for another degree or advanced certification program. Can you take one or two classes as a non-matriculated student before you commit to a program? Read the class descriptions and ask yourself if they sound interesting.

Stock up on recommended reading for leadership. Are you interested in or validated by what you read? Some of my favorite inspiring leadership books include the following:

- *Hacking Leadership: 10 Ways Great Leaders Inspire Learning That Teachers, Students, and Parents Love* by Joe Sanfelippo and Tony Sinanis
- *The One Thing: The Surprisingly Simple Truth behind Extraordinary Results* by Gary W. Keller and Jay Papasan
- *The Fifth Discipline* by Peter Senge
- *Leadership on the Line* by Ronald A. Heifetz and Marty Linsky
- *Change Leader: Learning to Do What Matters Most* by Michael Fullan
- *Reframing Organizations* by Lee G. Bolman and Terrence E. Deal
- Talk "off the record" to current leadership folks you trust. Ask them about the nuts and bolts of their daily responsibilities and how they felt during their transition to leadership.

- Participate in leadership chats on Twitter. Try to gauge the learning and experience of those currently in the position you aspire to.
- Search for potential jobs and note what intrigues you. Write your ideal job description and see if this position exists in your school or elsewhere.

REFLECTIONS FROM A "*WORK IN PROGRESS*"

Thirteen years of classroom teaching, and it's time to shake things up again. But I'm nervous. New opportunities are exciting, but they are also terrifying. I love teaching and am a good teacher, but I can do more and contribute to my school community differently. It's time for me to help others find their own successes as I have found mine.

I'm choosing a hybrid role as a classroom teacher and a teacher coach because the daily grind of an administrator's job isn't for me. Plus, I'm not sure I can be an effective coach without having one foot in the "teacher" role. I know many effective coaches don't teach anymore, but I need to stay relevant and have a space where teachers can see me engaging with the kids I have developed a relationship with—not just taking responsibilities for someone else's class for a period or two.

I'm already concerned with how my colleagues will treat me in this new role, so I need to maintain my credibility. I want them to know I am actually doing what I ask them to try. I believe in it, and I can model it. My greatest fear about this switch is the level of resistance to new ideas I may face from the teachers I want to help. I can easily get around resistance from the students I help, but adults have a harder time breaking habits, and they are often unwilling to try.

Making sure my pedagogy and approach are sound should reduce potential resistance and show teachers I'm eager to help them develop their skills.

As I grow in this new capacity, I'd like to . . .

- Develop a rapport with my colleagues so they trust my judgment and feel safe to take risks,

- Encourage teachers to visit my classroom so we can talk about what they want to try and change in their own classrooms,

- Listen to teachers' personal goals so my agenda doesn't impose on their growth,

- Be an unbiased observer to ensure I understand teacher strengths before helping them grow,

- Develop curriculum with my colleagues that puts students at the center of the learning environment, focusing strongly on a growth mindset rather than grades,

- Help implement a schoolwide shift away from traditional grading and support staff through this transition,

- Help integrate technology to support student learning and enrich student learning experiences, and

- Continue to work on my own pedagogy so I am growing as I help others.

Change is hard but worthwhile. I'm ready for this one!

Finding the Right New Job

If you love to teach as much as I do, making the decision to leave the classroom will never be easy. Even after you make the decision to leave, you may decide your heart still lives in the classroom. Keep in mind that no decision is permanent. You may want to go back to the classroom someday, so don't burn any bridges on your way out the door. But when you find the right position, you'll be challenged and feel rewarded by the move.

As I was evaluating a potential change, I created a job description of an ideal position, including a job proposal, proposed schedule, and proposed responsibilities. Taking time to consider these elements of a position helped me clarify what I was looking for. I focused heavily on the strengths used in the classroom that I could carry into leadership. You may find, as I did, a hybrid position is the right decision at first and then you can decide differently as you go.

POSITION PROPOSAL

If you want to make a career move, consider creating a position proposal based on your goals and credentials, such as the one shown on the next page.

POSITION PROPOSAL

Overview: Proposal is for a new position to aid in teacher development, technology integration, and whole-school assessment improvement from formative assessment creation to reflection and student empowerment. Schools considering a move to portfolio assessment and standards-based learning would be ideal.

Job title: Assessment and Accountability (Data) Coach

Job focus: Support school staff in developing assessment practices to empower students, improve learning, and aid teachers in their commitment to increase student engagement. Student-centered coaching will ensure data around student learning will drive instructional practices. Different protocols will be used to help develop student growth. Assessment and reflection practices will be embedded to ensure both students and teachers learn this better.

Job description: Support the school community to build a stronger understanding of effective alternative assessment practices. Assist teachers as they move away from traditional testing and grading and toward project-based learning with an emphasis on formative, actionable feedback and student voice/choice. Work with teachers to design projects around curriculum aligned with standards and offer areas of differentiation, helping to include students in this process as well.

Evaluation of the position: After each marking period, the coach will look at student data classroom practices along with teacher feedback. Administrators will be able to observe progress, discuss goals, and set benchmarks with the coach to be met over a period of time.

At the end of the year, success of the new assessment practices will be determined by student growth and overall community buy-in. A pre- and post-staff evaluation about the new assessment practices, co-constructed with administration, will be conducted to measure the coach's growth by measuring their growth.

Qualifications

- Fifteen(+) years in the classroom as a highly effective ELA and Journalism teacher
- Nationally board-certified in ELA
- Teacher coach with the UFT Teacher Center
- Experience working with administrators on school committees (leadership team, curriculum, accreditation, assessment, and portfolio) to help colleagues improve pedagogy for the benefit of student learning
- Author of eight education books on the topics of alternative assessment, student-centered learning, reflection/self-assessment, questioning, homework, peer feedback, and broader-range educational philosophy
- Blogger with *Education Week Teacher*
- Experience with technology integration in and out of the classroom
- Further credentials with my full résumé and references

PROPOSED SCHEDULE

As part of my proposal, I created a five-day schedule with eight periods a day. You can include flexibility in alternative job periods as needed. Lunch could also be flexible.

Monday	Tuesday	Wednesday
Newspaper class (teaching period)	Newspaper class (teaching period)	Newspaper class (teaching period)
Teacher meetings and visitations	Teacher meetings and visitations	Teacher meetings and visitations
Teacher meetings and visitations	Teacher meetings and visitations	Teacher meetings and visitations
Co-planning	Co-planning	Co-planning
Administrative duties	Administrative duties	Administrative duties
Lunch	Lunch	Lunch
Teacher meetings and visitations	Teacher meetings and visitations	Teacher meetings and visitations
Professional Development (PD) planning and reflection time	PD planning and reflection time	PD planning and reflection time

Thursday	Friday
Newspaper class (teaching period)	Newspaper class (teaching period)
Teacher meetings and visitations	Teacher meetings and visitations
Teacher meetings and visitations	Teacher meetings and visitations
Co-planning	Co-planning
Administrative duties	Administrative duties
Lunch	Lunch
Teacher meetings and visitations	Teacher meetings and visitations
PD planning and reflection time	PD planning and reflection time

REVIEW THE PROPOSED RESPONSIBILITIES, POSSIBLE ACTIVITIES, AND BENEFITS AND OUTCOMES

Responsibilities: Teacher Model—lab site

(This could potentially be a newspaper class or some kind of journalism class resulting in an online student media outlet.)

Activities

- Visit teachers
- Debrief pedagogy
- Conduct student interviews
- Share lessons and units
- Plan strategies
- Allow for teacher observations

Benefits and Outcomes

- Display best practices in action
- Offer a working model for teachers, outside pedagogues, and administrators to visit to view tech integration and no-grades environment

Responsibilities: Teacher Coach

Activities

- Target teachers in need
- Informally visit with teachers
- Provide feedback and strategies
- Assist and support teachers with tech reflection and no-grades integration
- Help develop curriculum and assessment design for the entire school

Benefits and Outcomes

- Help align school vision
- Help develop pedagogy
- Provide a better, streamlined environment for student learning
- Develop individual teacher voice

Responsibilities: Co-planning and Team Teaching

Activities

- Help implement strategies by pushing into classes of teachers
- Help develop student-centered activities to engage all learners
- Focus on student voice and involvement in the process

Benefits and Outcomes

- Support coached teachers by following through on the strategies in and out of the classroom

Responsibilities: Data Gathering and Analysis

Activities

- Review observations to target teachers in need
- Track progress of teacher with student data and outcomes

Benefits and Outcomes

- Ensure strategies are working
- Develop plans and accountability

Responsibilities: Professional Learning Provider and Planner

Activities

- Poll staff regularly for areas of need
- Coordinate book groups
- Plan specialized professional development sessions for the whole school or small groups based on needs
- Plan EdCamp-style professional development once a month to make use of staff expertise
- Develop school-wide understanding of student-centered assessment and reasons for moving away from traditional grading
- Promote a portfolio culture where learning is shown through the process over time rather than just in summative exams
- Support teachers as they help students communicate their learning better
- Teach classes on specific tech to promote project-based learning
- Promote reflection for both teachers and students

Benefits and Outcomes

- Ensure the needs of all teachers and learners are met
- Continue to support a wider effort to develop teaching strategies, including technology integration, to ensure enriched student learning

By taking the time to fully realize what I wanted to do and commit it to writing, I was able to focus personally before making any decisions. While this specific proposal never materialized, the first part-time teaching position I took was a hybrid instructional coach/teacher position similar to the one above.

Once I was clear about what I wanted to do, the aspects of the job I loved and wanted to keep growing in, and where I wanted to grow, I was able to articulate these in interviews; furthermore, while it may seem crazy, knowing and articulating what I wanted seemed to make it available once I put it into the universe. Ultimately, the teaching/coaching position through the Teacher Center offered a new perspective and new responsibilities. I still taught three classes, but I also ran a teacher's center, taught professional development, visited teachers' classrooms, and provided feedback.

No decision involving change comes without trade-offs. Life shifts, and what you want and where you want to go often changes with it. Perhaps your building administrator suggests you take the next step, or you fill in for someone in an interim position. Your path to leadership may be very different from mine. As long as you have clarity and understand decisions aren't permanent, you can take the leap with confidence.

REFLECTIONS FROM A "*WORK IN PROGRESS*"

Every teacher is a leader in his own right, but leading teachers and growing their talent is more nuanced than leading students. After spending sixteen years in the classroom cultivating a deep respect for the learning process and growth mindset of "my kids," I've learned to let go and let them lead while artfully addressing needs and concerns, invisibly, from a position of expertise. I've intentionally placed them in charge in a system historically telling them to be compliant if they want to be successful.

Like our students, teachers tend to remain compliant to their administrators when their school culture doesn't allow for creativity or risk taking. But if leaders are going to successfully grow teacher talent to maximize the most student-learning success, they must empower teachers to feel confident enough to compel students to take risks too.

Asking people to take risks but not supporting them adequately presents only empty words. Risk taking and change-making are scary, and doing them successfully makes a big mess. I'm learning that confident leaders expect the mess and encourage it—and even stick around to help turn it into something beautiful.

Pointing out the mess is easy, but what good does just pointing it out do? Risk takers will ultimately feel alienated and likely will stop taking risks. Plus, when leaders point out the mess, they're sending mixed messages. They shouldn't tell folks to take risks and then beat them down after they do; instead, leaders should partner with teachers to reflect on what went well and where adjustments can be made to make the mess into a masterpiece.

As I shift into the position of partner, I need to remember I'm not just thinking about my classroom and my students anymore; I must think more globally. What will benefit the teachers I will be working with? Recently I got some good advice: Be intentional and invisible in the way I carry out initiatives. I'm not here to fix teachers; rather, I want to help develop the skills they already possess by having them set goals while working with them to achieve the goals.

After watching and experiencing many different leadership styles, I know how I hope to be and how I don't want to be.

To exemplify the global leadership I plan to execute, I will need to be . . .

- Knowledgeable, but humble,
- A truly good listener who engages in dialogue and asks a lot of questions—and makes eye contact,
- Visibly present—face-to-face and available via technology,
- A model of the expectation—showing more than one way to do things,
- Transparent—admitting when I don't know something and eager to work with the team to find solutions,
- Ethical—shedding light, rather than shadows, wherever possible—maintaining my integrity,
- Aware of my mistakes and eager to correct them,
- Collaborative—working with others because we are better together than individually,
- A decision maker who can make effective choices in a pinch but also knows when to slow down and not react, and
- Patient—some challenges take time, and although I will want to quickly improve things, fast doesn't always achieve what is needed.

When Switching Roles Is Not Your Choice

Many people don't choose to be new leaders or leaders in training. Often *their* leaders empower them or strongly suggest they move into a leadership position. You might be flattered if someone has made this suggestion to you, but remember that your career is up to *you*. No one can force you into a position you don't want. If your supervisor is a strong leader, he or she will know this.

Being encouraged to take the leap is very different from being placed in a position you didn't sign up for. If you find yourself working through a formal leadership program you feel you were forced into, take time to reflect whether this is where you *want* to be. Passion for your career and calling is what keeps you on this path. Veering down a path that doesn't entice you the way your current position does may be a recipe for disaster. Keep your eyes and heart open. Only you can make the ultimate decision about where you end up.

Daily Reflections for Change

As you consider moving into leadership, take a moment to reflect on what you've read and on the following questions:

- ☐ Where you are currently on your journey?
- ☐ What is prompting you to think about moving to another position?
- ☐ If you are exhibiting any of the signs mentioned above, how long have you felt this way?
- ☐ What are your current options for change?
- ☐ How would you describe your ideal job?

CHAPTER 2

Teacher Leadership as a Precursor to School Leadership

IF YOUR ACTIONS INSPIRE OTHERS TO DREAM MORE, LEARN MORE, DO MORE, AND BECOME MORE, YOU ARE A LEADER.

—President John Quincy Adams

Teachers *are* leaders. They work with kids every day, often having to wrangle the most challenging students, and they work to ensure each child's success. Teachers demonstrate leadership daily whether you call it *leadership* or not. My experience as a master teacher has served me well in both teacher leadership and now in curriculum and instructional leadership. Adult learners, of course, are very different from student learners, and as you move into a position in which you are leading adults, you need to be ready for what this job will entail.

Preparing for Leadership

While leadership books outline specific characteristics of a good leader, and being prepared as a leader is definitely helpful, I don't believe there is one perfect kind of leader. Just like with teaching, finding the right fit for your leadership style is important. When you begin to interview for leadership positions, consider the job description and ask a lot of questions about the school culture and needs, to make sure the job is a good fit. Even if the fit is perfect, you will face challenges; if the fit isn't right, they will be exponentially greater.

As you prepare to make a change, take on more responsibilities in your current job. Ask to attend professional development to help you grow your content or pedagogical expertise, then share your learning with your administration and colleagues. *Before* administration asks for volunteers, offer to lead a committee related to a change you'd like to see in your school. Attend board meetings or other open meetings available in your district or read the meeting minutes if you can't be present. Be the first to put your hat in the ring for any new opportunities:

- Get involved in hiring committees, listening to what your administrator asks and says about each candidate.
- Attend parent association meetings. Get to know the leadership and assist them as they support the school.
- Help revise current policies (e.g., assessment or lateness).
- Lead a colleague circle or a book group to improve the culture or instructional practice.
- Volunteer to coordinate a professional learning day or a meeting around a topic you feel well versed in.
- Start writing a blog about your experiences and get connected on Twitter to learn from other people in your position.
- Apply to present at local, regional, or national conferences on topics important to you.

- Attend conferences to learn about specific areas you want to grow in.
- Lead focus groups with students and colleagues to better understand where change is needed.
- Volunteer to do Board of Education presentations on school-wide initiatives.

The amount of learning available through these kinds of experiences will help prepare you for leadership. Take advantage of opportunities to lead groups, particularly those where change can be spearheaded. Doing so is great practice for a full-leadership position.

Putting Classroom Experience into Practice in Other Areas

As a teacher, you already possess leadership qualities. Your classroom experiences serve you well, particularly in honing communication skills. Consider your ability to get to know the needs of your students and the ways you differentiate learning for them. You can apply this skill to understand the needs of adult learners also. You want them to feel empowered and take ownership of their learning the same way your students do. Communication is key to ensure you know the people you are working with. Make sure you have clear lines of conversation and that teachers know how best to reach you (e.g., email or phone). When you need something, be direct, but know how each of your learners hears feedback best. Be sure to employ that knowledge in how to best get your point across. Learners, regardless of their ages, have specific needs to optimize their growth potential. Reading the people you are working with and providing them with what they need (especially when they don't recognize it themselves) will be essential.

Some of the best professional development I have experienced in my teacher leadership roles was focused on the differences between teaching student and adult learners. Understanding that change needs to be approached differently and that expertise needs to be harnessed when it comes to working with adults is important. Adult learners—like student learners—need to feel valued, but tempering the way you involve colleagues and team members sets the tone for any potential growth.

REFLECTIONS FROM A "*WORK IN PROGRESS*"

I always find it hard to receive compliments, even though deep down I'm proud of what I have accomplished. I work hard and persevere, and given the amount of effort and passion I've expended over the last few years honing my craft and shifting my mindset, I appreciate others noticing.

Knowing my process, however, and considering the new adventures and challenges before me, I've been eliciting advice from people I respect and admire to help me understand and develop into the role I am taking on. Although I know a lot, there is much I still need to learn to be as effective in my new job as I was in my old one; however, I am certain of several things:

- All people are learners first. Adults and children are learners with lifelong learning expectations.

- With humility and pride, I ask a million questions, hear varied answers, and use my own experience and expertise to make decisions.

- As the new person in a traditional school culture, the most important thing I can do is listen. As I get to know my role and my staff, I'll better understand what has been in place, make some mental notes, and be cautious about sharing potential changes.

- I'm a transparent and public entity, so my staff probably knows more about me, if they took the time to look, than I know about them. Like I said earlier, though I'm proud of what I know, I don't plan to lead with it. It's there, and it will come in handy eventually, but right now it's sitting on the bookshelf (literally and figuratively).

- Shifting my mindset away from being a classroom teacher to being a collaborative leader is going to take meditation every day. Although being in a leadership role—in action and in title—is different and my relationships with people will reflect this, it doesn't have to be negative.

- Although I won't have students of my own, all the students are mine to share. I love children and working with them. They're one of the reasons I became a teacher. So I plan to be around them a lot.

- I will never forget what it feels like to be a classroom teacher. As such, I would never ask my staff to do something I wouldn't do myself. Every choice I make as a leader is to benefit our kids. Ultimately, as kids change, so must the teacher's craft. When changes are expected, I will do my very best to make sure they are meaningful and supported.

- I will make many mistakes, but I'm not afraid, because they are opportunities for amazing growth. I will stay transparent about my missteps and worries, modeling to my staff that this is the only way to grow. I'm committed to learning from my mistakes to be a better leader.

- As I learn from what is currently happening at my school and the mission of my district, I will create—with my staff—a space that truly integrates learning in a meaningful way. Ideas and growth don't happen in isolation; therefore, my team must be cohesive and grow together.

- I will constantly reflect on the personal learning and on-the-job expertise I gain, confidently intermingling what I know as an educator with the best practices for my role as a director.

- I won't get everything done all the time, but I will accomplish what needs to be finished and will do it right since this is more important than just getting it done.

- I want my passion and enthusiasm about learning to be visible, infectious, and inspiring—not intimidating—so I can develop the necessary relationships to help grow the programs I'm involved with.

- I'm experiencing a lot of change, but it is good; in fact, it's the one constant I have.

So I launch myself into this new year with quiet confidence, humility, and pride. I'll lead with my open heart and mind, certain I'll experience a tremendous amount of growth this year.

I was reminded this year of something I learned in my teacher leadership roles: Teachers want to be heard and appreciated. Forcing new ideas or initiatives on folks before they are ready will result in almost certain failure. So pace yourself. Survey your group anonymously to get a better understanding of them. Always ask for honest feedback, and more importantly, listen to it, reflect on it, and respond to it. Nothing is worse than discounting ideas elicited from others; it's a surefire way to make your team resent you.

Finding a Program Addressing Your Needs

Most leadership positions require a certification or degree, which necessitates additional schooling. While this experience can be humbling, it is also beneficial because it reconnects you to being a student; additionally, although your teaching experience gets you to a certain point, you can't discount the benefit of specific training and learning on any areas not essential or even related to your current job.

When you start to research the program you need, think about what's most important to you. For me, the "most important" was finding a program allowing me to start my job without having the required certification. Ironically, my path to leadership was the same one I took when I started teaching. The job I wanted became available, but my credentials didn't meet the needs of the position. Rather than count myself out, though, I found an alternative solution to remain a viable candidate and get the certification I needed. In order for me to accept my new job, I had to do the following:

- Develop a portfolio exemplifying my current leadership experience and submit it to the program, which later submitted it to the State with a recommendation
- Pass the state certification exams for school district leaders *before* starting my program coursework
- Obtain recommendations from colleagues and bosses
- Submit an application to the program
- Start my classes right away
- Work directly with a mentor who would guide me and teach me on-the-job skills

After finding the program that was right for me, I was able to start my job and go to school at the same time, fulfilling my new leadership responsibilities with the help of an on-site mentor.

As you search for potential programs, keep the following in mind:

- Know what certification or degree is needed for your new position.
- Go on your state's education website to find programs offered locally that satisfy your requirements.
- Most leadership programs are offered in cohorts, so timing is important. Get into a program *before* it is necessary. It's better to be in a program and not need it than to foolishly wait until the last minute, like I did.
- Make phone calls and talk to advisors who will best direct you as you decide.
- Stay in touch with the potential program and your potential position to share information and make better decisions.
- If money is an issue, you don't have to go to private institutions though they may offer more convenient online options. Some schools offer "hybrid" weekend classes, meaning students meet for three Saturdays and complete work and interact with class members online. Loans are usually available through state agencies. Be sure to speak to the financial aid office at the institution you will be attending.
- Check out timelines and class schedules if you have a limited amount of time.
- Once you make a decision on a program, consult with your advisor to make arrangements to get started when you need to.
- Track and manage your coursework and requirements so you don't prolong your needed graduation date.

Once you decide on and start a program, give it your all. No one is going to be tracking your progress, and you will get out of your learning experience what you put into it. Having originally complained about needing this program to do my job, now—a little over a year later—I am almost finished and am grateful for the learning experience. I took law class and finance class, filling in a definite gap in my own knowledge base. I worked hard, reading ahead, reflecting on assignments, and continuously applying what I was learning. Going into a leadership program definitely added value for me. Not only did I gain from the reading and teaching of my classes, I've also become a better new leader because of the expertise and philosophy of my professors and the perspectives and experiences of my cohorts.

REFLECTIONS FROM A "*WORK IN PROGRESS*"

I don't believe any child could have enjoyed being in school more than I did. I felt a special kind of adrenaline when I stepped into a new class, soaking up context clues and information about the rules. Once I was oriented, I knew I would experience the exciting rush of learning new content and skills as I worked toward my coveted "A." When I moved into college, I loved the anxious thrill of choosing a class and making my mark in it.

By the time grad school rolled around, my interest in learning had begun to change. I had started my teaching journey by this time, and I needed practical learning to ensure I was effective in my classroom. And now I face another change. After teaching for sixteen years and helping so many students and colleagues rethink what acquiring knowledge looks like, I'm intimidated to step back into a classroom after my own learning hiatus. Sure, I've been to conferences and had professional learning opportunities directly or indirectly aligned with what I was doing in the classroom. But those weren't the same as going back to school.

As I prepare for my next job, I'm moving into uncharted waters. School wasn't on my radar before this summer, and I've felt completely out of my element walking onto a new campus and enrolling in my first leadership class; I've even felt physically sick. The idea of school excites me, but sitting in a class with complete strangers in a content area outside my field of expertise is scary. I think about how my students must feel when they step into their new classes—especially mine.

I don't want to monopolize the learning space. I want to listen instead to my classmates and take in what I am here to learn. I'm here as an equal—not focused on my long teaching experience or the many books I've written. If I walked into class thinking I knew it all, I'd simply miss too many learning opportunities.

So I arrived at class early on the first day and tried to settle in. As my peers came in, I observed and quietly kept to myself because I'm painfully shy, especially when I'm in a situation where people don't know who I am or why I'm there. It was a while before I opened up in class. Like one of my more reticent students, I needed some small-group discussions and writing before I could share my ideas openly. After being in the class for several hours and getting to share my ideas with others, my confidence about learning started to come back. I wasn't feeling as nervous about sharing my ideas or about doing an assignment incorrectly. I like the anonymity of being in the class and can't wait to start getting into the work.

If I want to be a leader, I must model the behaviors I expect my students and colleagues to exemplify. This means connecting with them in a vulnerable and meaningful way. I must also listen, take in what I need from other smart people around me, and collaborate effectively to do what's best for my school community.

In order to be successful in my new position, I have a lot of new information to learn and apply. So with excitement, I eagerly approach the new material and my future colleagues with an open heart and mind. After all, we are all in education for the same reason—to make it better for all kids.

Daily Reflections for Change

- ☐ What role(s), beyond being a teacher, do you play or have you played in your school?
- ☐ What leadership skills have you developed in these roles, making you a good candidate for a leadership position?
- ☐ In what areas of leadership do you need more professional learning? Where might you get it?
- ☐ Have you considered an online leadership program or one at a local institution?
- ☐ What fears or challenges might you face going back to school in your current life situation? How might you overcome those obstacles?

CHAPTER 3

The Ache of the Shift

TAKE CHANCES, MAKE MISTAKES. THAT'S HOW YOU
GROW. PAIN NOURISHES YOUR COURAGE. YOU HAVE
TO FAIL IN ORDER TO PRACTICE BEING BRAVE.

—Mary Tyler Moore

This is how I would describe my first month as a new school leader. Despite the fact I hadn't yet comprehended the full job description or my daily routine, I smiled my way through a lot of discomfort and blissful unawareness. I had a mentor who was readily available to answer questions, but if I had no questions to ask, I became very aware of the void that had been created inside of me by not being in the classroom.

For sixteen years my identity had been built on my growth as a classroom educator, my passion for the content I taught, and the connections and relationships I had established with my students and colleagues. Much like grades had defined me as a smart student (or so I thought), this combination of growth, content, and relationships had defined me as an effective teacher and had established a familiar routine I wasn't sure how to replace.

The Inevitable Regret

After spending years cultivating a teaching career, I went through a mourning period—a daily reminder and regret about choosing to walk away from the love that never disappointed me enough to break up with it in a fit of anger. I hadn't fallen out of love with teaching; we had simply started moving on different paths, and so it was time.

For a while, I felt a longing and nostalgia about the classroom—a "revisionist" memory of only the good days. My new position had an extremely hard time competing with these recollections. But I'm tenacious and knew I had to allow myself time to mourn the loss of the classroom. I could then rebrand my decision as an *extension* of my teaching career and not as a *replacement* of it.

People had told me missing my old job when I first switched positions was normal, but after a year in the new position, I still missed teaching. Thankfully, I found ways to keep what I loved most about the classroom and channel what I was missing into my new position. If you're facing this situation, consider any of these suggestions:

- Conduct tons of classroom walkthroughs to watch learning— *not* to evaluate the teachers on your team—to determine if learning and goals are being addressed and to connect with teachers and students. The more you are in classrooms, the more you can catch "awesome" happening.
- Participate in school events and activities like field trips and clubs. I went to newspaper meetings and provided feedback to students about their writing. I also shared my knowledge with the teachers and participated in the experience.

- Be involved in classroom celebrations, a low-stakes way to get into classrooms and be around kids—and teachers—in their glory moments. Watching students present their learning in a variety of ways is a great way to connect, be in the classroom, and build relationships with students.
- Plan with teachers and offer to co-teach when it is appropriate. This is another low-stakes way to be in the classroom and build credibility with your team. How many times has a team leader offered to participate with you in this way, but never followed through? Be the leader who makes the offer—*and* does it. It will benefit the teacher, the students, and you. Plus, word spreads quickly, and this can open doors to more classrooms and more students.
- Model expectations by being a guest teacher where appropriate. When co-planning isn't appropriate, maybe you can model a lesson or be a guest reader in a class. This way the teacher can watch you and you can interact with the students as the teacher rather than as an outsider.

Isolation

Another challenge I faced as a new leader was isolation. As a teacher, I wasn't isolated; I was still a part of a unit. My colleagues and I may not have always agreed, but we were "in it together," and I had my group of friends who made the school days easier.

The first September and October in my new position were lonely months. I still didn't know whom I could trust, and because I was so new, and no one else was experiencing this with me, I felt lonely. I was getting to know people and starting to build relationships, but my office felt confining—almost like a prison. Even on my loneliest days as a teacher, I always had my students, and they had never let me down.

Although most school districts have a unit of administration, the dynamics of mine are different. My district has only a few administrators, and only one or two of my peers reside even remotely close to my office. As a result, reaching out to those who understand my vulnerable place requires a phone call or additional effort to get to their offices.

In these isolated moments, I reached out to my PLN (professional learning network) for support. These were my close friends with whom I had grown my career—people who saw me simply as "Starr," the person. They were the sounding board and safe haven I needed. I received day-to-day help from my mentor and some colleagues who had been leaders slightly longer than I had been. But I also needed support from friends—the people who knew me and always told me what I needed to hear. In the early months of your first leadership position, especially if you are in a new school or district, you will likely need to reach outside for this kind of support.

The isolation of the early months was almost worse than missing the kids. This loneliness often made me question my decision. But I'm not a quitter. I held on and worked hard to make friends, testing the waters to measure how much I could share and with whom. Frankly, I found this exhausting. I'm not a game player and am transparent beyond a normal level. So I had to learn to protect myself and share less, even though it wasn't what I wanted.

Being One of *Them*

As a new team leader, you will definitely experience isolation. For the most part it will continue because you are no longer part of *us*. Now you are one of *them*—like a Sith from the Dark Side coming to ruin everyone's life. When I became a new leader, my teacher colleagues said I had gone to the "dark side," but I beg to differ. Leadership doesn't have to be the dark side. It can be light, optimistic, and supportive, but it definitely takes time to get your team to believe you aren't one of *them*.

I realized early on that my team was accustomed to working with leaders who were very different from me. As a matter of fact, since many on my team have been teaching in the district for more than twenty years, they have experienced many leaders, all telling them different ways to do things and creating various priority lists. It quickly became evident I couldn't be a leader who just told my team what to do, giving one directive after another. I had to be a leader who listened and tried my best to present change in a palatable way—and initially only where it was necessary even if I wanted to do more.

Be Transparent

If you are going to overcome the "us versus them" mentality, you must be transparent. Every decision you make and every idea you share must be done honestly and clearly. This year I learned to lead with the *reason* and come back to the *what*. Reminding teachers that ideas or changes won't be imminent or done without proper implementation plans is also helpful.

When I introduce a new idea, instead of just presenting research and having a discussion, I remind my team no change is coming tomorrow. I want them to think about what they read and how it resonates with current practice and then consider how a small shift could improve learning for all. If some feel the shift is large instead of small and not aligned philosophically with their experiences, I want to hear more about what is challenging for them and better understand and support them in any way I can.

Often in our department meetings, I present ideas and take data from what I hear in small-group discussions. At the end of each meeting, I put together a short Google form to get their feedback. I look forward to their feedback, and I always read it, even if it isn't positive—maybe especially if it isn't positive. Either way, the feedback is a way to expand the conversation, see where we are as a group, and make necessary adjustments—similar to what I would do after a lesson in my classroom.

Organizing Your Time as a New Leader

One challenge to get used to as a new leader is the fact that school bells no longer dictate when you can go to the bathroom or do your job. Yes, the bells still ring, but you aren't planning your life around them unless you are co-teaching or holding meetings with teachers.

The best thing you can do is know the bell schedules for the schools you are responsible for but plan your schedule in a calendar—not by the bells. In our district, the kindergarten center and elementary schools function on different time schedules. Being aware of these schedules helps me plan my time, which is essential to my being productive and efficient in my new job, just as it was when planning for my classroom.

Bear in mind, regardless of how much you plan, you should be prepared to address unexpected issues more pressing than what you have scheduled. Be ready with a "Plan B" in the event your day changes unexpectedly.

REFLECTIONS FROM A "*WORK IN PROGRESS*"

Scheduling myself and being productive are some of my strengths. My colleagues and friends have always looked to me for guidance on organizing their time better to be more efficient, and I've always been able to help. Ironically, however, managing my time is one of the challenges I've had since starting my new position.

As a teacher, I followed a rigid schedule signified by the school bells. Based on the bells, I compartmentalized my working hours into blocks of forty-one to forty-four minutes, helping me distinguish when I was teaching and when I could work on other professional duties.

Another huge difference is my commute. I'm a morning person, and over the years, I've become accustomed to waking up between 4:00 and 5:00 a.m., being on the road no later than 5:30, and starting my work day promptly at 6:30. While I had to personally sacrifice seeing my son off in the morning, I got to work early and was able to prepare myself for the day. This also alleviated the amount of work I had to bring home in the evening. Since I now live less than five miles from my new district, I'm able to get Logan on the bus every day, but I get to work later, so I'm looking for a new routine.

While I have many clocks in my new office, I don't look at them often, because I'm constantly absorbed in my work. Whether I'm writing observations, emailing, or reading, I'm always busy. There never seems to be enough time in a day to do anything. This is problematic because I'm not taking care of myself—a bad habit I'm working to change. It is very easy to get consumed by meetings, walkthroughs, planning, and deadlines, so it is necessary to plan breaks and make time to clear your head.

To get the most out of my day without burning out, I plan to do the following:

- Create a schedule for each day—the day before. In addition to scheduled meetings on my calendar, I'll add a concrete list of goals. As I accomplish each goal, I will cross it off and move through the list.

- Set alerts on my phone to remind myself to take needed breaks to eat and move around.

> • Remind myself it is okay if I don't get through everything on the list every day.
>
> As a highly efficient person who prides herself on getting things done excellently, I have a hard time allowing myself not to be productive. I may need to redefine what "productive" looks and sounds like. I have plenty of evidence to support what it looks like in the classroom, but it's time to start building experience in my new field.

Professional Dress and Professional Behavior

As petty as it sounds, the change to more professional dress was one of the hardest parts of the new job for me to adjust to early on. As a classroom teacher, I often wore comfortable, dressed-down clothes that made moving around a busy classroom easier. My wash-and-wear wardrobe also spared me the expense of dry cleaning more business-like attire. Certainly, I dressed more professionally for parent/teacher conferences, but I came to work each day ready to get my hands dirty.

When I arrived at my new school, I wanted to make a positive impression, especially since so many unknowns were already working against me. Plus, I look younger than I am and have many visible tattoos, so I was concerned about the expectations and judgment of the staff I'd be leading and the colleagues with whom I'd be working.

My bravado has always been that it doesn't matter what I look like; what matters is how well I do my job. I had therefore always justified not wearing business attire, because it didn't feel appropriate or accessible to my New York City students, who were largely seniors in high school. Suddenly I was working in the suburbs with teachers who had been in the district almost double the length of my career, and I knew there was a benefit to looking the part. I can't walk in heels, so I purchased many pairs of flats and committed to wearing dresses or skirt suits most days. When it was appropriate, I dressed down in a school polo and khakis and, as I eased into my role, I felt more comfortable exposing the tattoos on my arms and dying my hair purple.

My best advice as you move into leadership is this: Observe your new location. Ask your direct supervisor and new colleagues about proper dress protocols and follow them. Once folks get to know you better, you can find where you are comfortable within the realm of your new culture. In order to do your job well, you need to be comfortable. So find a way to respect the culture while being true to yourself and—most of all—functional.

Dealing with New Tasks

When you walk into a new situation, you face new experiences. If you're lucky, something from your former positions will help inform you how to proceed, but it's important to know whom to ask for different kinds of help. Thankfully, a lot of people will be able to help you.

As you're getting familiar, start noting your gaps in knowledge and who may be your go-to person to fill them. This needs analysis will help you stay ahead of potential chaos.

As you consider what you need to know in your new position . . .

- Ask a lot of questions of folks who have been in the school for a while.
- If you have access to the person who was in your position before, use him or her as a resource.
- Observe as much as you can, using all the information at your fingertips; for example, the printed school calendar offers a lot of information about upcoming events possibly important to your particular job. Ask questions ahead of time.

- When something does surprise you the first time, make a note to ensure you don't make the same error next year. Be proactive and create reminders in your online calendar or appointment book to ensure you're prepared.

REFLECTIONS FROM A "*WORK IN PROGRESS*"

Who knew when I stepped into my new position I would have so many hidden corners to explore? I suppose leaders who have held their positions for a long time could be chuckling at me because they know the secret spots.

Being responsible for four departments that are beginning to function as a cohesive whole—while I'm still learning the ropes—has been an adventure. Every day I discover something new. Until I am actually involved in a task, I can't wrap my brain around the depth and scope of what is expected.

As light begins to shine on my new learning, I'm reminded of being in the classroom where my most memorable, important, and meaningful learning experiences were the ones I explored and discovered on my own. While there were expectations and standards, I wanted to exceed them. Ultimately, I got to mastery through doing.

Too often I forget that learning—in the classroom and in life— happens in moments when I am forced to figure things out. My new role is one of these moments. I must first acknowledge I don't have all the answers, then I need to know where to find them. Some answers may come from human resources after I've developed more relationships with more people and asked a lot of questions. Others may come after I read and explore further on my own.

> *Too often I forget that learning—in the classroom and in life—happens in moments when I am forced to figure things out.*

The folks I'm working with are amazing and patient, eager to help me settle in and get acclimated. I'm grateful because I still have so much to learn. I hope I'm modeling a growth mindset, confident of what I bring to the table but also showing I'm not afraid to take a risk and be a learner. I am a learner first, exploring dark corners and shedding light on what once wasn't known or understood. I find this learning my greatest journey; I wake up invigorated about the adventures yet to come. I have a lot more to discover, and I'm eager to continue to collaborate with my colleagues so the kids can get what they need.

The more you exhibit the behaviors you'd like to see, the more likely they will become part of the culture, so aim high, ask for help, and don't fear the inevitable scrapes. They go away, but your experience and new knowledge will inform your future leaps.

Daily Reflections for Change

☐ What do you miss most—or fear you'll miss most—about being in the classroom?

☐ In your daily work, how have you remedied the deficit of not being in the classroom?

☐ In what areas can you do better to ensure your relevance in the classroom?

☐ In your current position, whom can you connect with as an honest sounding board?

☐ What structures have you put into place to ensure you are getting work done while staying excited about the work?

CHAPTER 4

Building Relationships for Early Success

> **TRUST IS THE GLUE OF LIFE. IT'S THE MOST ESSENTIAL INGREDIENT IN EFFECTIVE COMMUNICATION. IT'S THE FOUNDATIONAL PRINCIPLE THAT HOLDS ALL RELATIONSHIPS.**
>
> –Stephen Covey

*I*n education, relationships are everything. No exaggeration. People say it over and over again, but until you find yourself in a new position, you can easily underestimate the power of relationships. Doing so, however, would be foolish. Behind every successful leader is a person who knows and values the relationships he has built with every person in the organization. When you're in a new position, speaking to as many people as possible and developing genuine interest and trust with them, developing and supporting those relationships will increase your level of success and happiness in your position.

Find One Friend as Quickly as Possible

As I mentioned earlier, being a leader can be lonely. Finding your first real friend will ease some of the isolation. Seek out a person who is also in a leadership position, as he or she can empathize with your challenges. That said, anyone you can genuinely connect with and build an authentic trust with will be integral in your early days.

I had a mentor with whom I could share my challenges and ask for guidance, but I didn't consider him a "friend." I never wanted to share my insecurities or complaints with him. He was also my superior, and I worried about the impression I would make if I shared too much. This was a change coming from my experience as a teacher, when I had deep friendships with a number of colleagues. We had shared celebrations, frustrations, and even students, providing ample opportunities for us to honestly open up to each other about gripes or successes we may have had.

I longed for that kind of connection in my new role as a leader and tried to make them with members of my team. As much as I wanted to fit in with my new colleagues, the fact that I identified so much with being a classroom teacher proved to be a barrier.

A few very kind teachers sought me out, although I couldn't share deeply about my challenges, because I never wanted to make them feel uncomfortable. This would have been unfair of me regardless of how much I longed for their friendship. Over time, many teachers shared information with me about their personal and professional lives. I appreciated and valued this information because I wanted to know the folks on our team to be able to better help them.

When you're in a new position, many things feel unfamiliar. Being able to confide in someone who has been at the new location longer will help you maintain perspective in important ways. Be careful not to choose the wrong person, though. You need a trustworthy confidante. In my effort to make friends and fit in readily, at times I put my trust in people who hadn't earned it. I shared too much, too fast, and later regretted it. Because I second-guessed myself, I worried about the judgment of my peers, and this didn't help my ability to make good decisions. As you work to build friendships in your new job, consider these suggestions:

- Be cautiously optimistic.
- It's okay to be outgoing, but you don't have to share everything right away. Make sure to carefully consider the people you work with.
- Trust your instincts about people, but remember, many people have a personal agenda. This was hard for me to accept because I don't function this way. I discovered my level of transparency is hard for some people, and honesty is hard for others. In my old teaching roles, I was able to blog about everything that happened in my classroom, the flattering and the not so flattering. This public space was where I did my reflecting, and I was unashamed to share my experiences. I'm learning most people don't function this way.
- Talk to someone initially whom you trust even if it is someone outside of work; in fact, this might be best, especially for negative or challenging feelings.
- Fight the urge to gossip. Participating in unproductive and salacious discussions is always detrimental. It isn't friendship, and it won't help you get your job done well. It will only give you a false and temporary sense of fitting in.

Do Lots of Walkthroughs

To counter the "gotcha" mentality that most teachers will feel the first, second, or third time you are in their rooms, make being visible part of what you do. Getting into classrooms is a great way to learn about the folks on your team, meet students, and develop relationships with teachers whom you want to trust you.

Getting into classrooms gives you an opportunity to notice all the good things going on while noting things you'd like to change. Always go into rooms with a smile on your face and make sure to follow up afterward with a note or an email saying something specific about what you saw. Initially, keep these notes positive, saying something genuine about what you saw. These notes are an entry point to a much larger conversation transpiring over time. Teachers need to see you are on their side. They need to know you see their hard work and you want to help. Giving them positive feedback when you are in their spaces informally is a way to build capital with your team. Not only do you prove you know what you are doing, you also have an opportunity to show them you notice their great work. Because teachers aren't recognized positively enough, this is a benefit to them *and* to you.

Depending on your school's culture, find out how each teacher likes to be recognized. I learned the hard that way some teachers don't want public recognition, so using social media for them is a no-no. But sharing best practices you see in classrooms in a weekly or monthly newsletter is likely a great way to amplify what you are seeing.

REFLECTIONS FROM A "*WORK IN PROGRESS*"

As I peeked into the classroom of excited seventh-grade Spanish students, I couldn't help smiling widely. They were sitting in pairs with the Chromebooks on their desks, talking about the research they were doing. Spanish music played in the background. I smiled at the teacher, who had previously told me about the project, and eagerly joined the classroom, briskly walking to the side of the room with my notebook and making sure it was okay for me to start talking to the kids.

Kneeling down next to one group of boys, I asked what they were learning.

"We each have to research a Spanish-speaking country and talk about its influence on the United States."

"Cool! What country are each of you working on, and what have you learned so far?"

"Puerto Rico, the Dominican Republic, Mexico, and Venezuela."

Not so coincidentally, they all liked learning about the food best.

I made my way around and noticed the teacher was busy moving around the room, answering questions, and helping the students. Clearly, everyone was having a good time and learning.

I was reminded again how much I missed being in the classroom. While I knew the transition would be challenging, the part of being a teacher hardest to let go of is the students and watching them learn while actively participating in their discovery.

As I continue to design what my days look like, I've made a conscious effort to get into classrooms daily to celebrate what teachers do well and observe student learning. Although I'm not sure yet if my teachers will take me up on it, I've offered to come into classrooms to teach lessons, be an extra set of eyes, celebrate their achievements, or do anything else to show them I am willing to be present in this experience with them.

While I spend no more than eight minutes in a class, what I've loved most about doing walkthroughs is observing student learning and the rapport students have with their teachers. I walk into every classroom expecting to see what teachers do to make their kids want to come back tomorrow.

As I leave the classroom, I smile and thank the teacher if it isn't a disruption. Later I write the teacher a thank-you note including something specific I enjoyed or something especially helpful for the students. It's extremely important my teachers know I'm there to support them and work with them to build better learning environments for the students. I don't want them to feel anxious when they see me come in; I want them to feel good.

All of this is a precursor to formal observations and the best way to ensure they are meaningful. I want teachers to continue to reflect on their goals and areas they are working on and let me know about them so I can provide specific feedback the way I did with the students in my classroom. Positive, sincere,

Positive, sincere, and specific feedback is a powerful tool to let teachers know I see—and appreciate—what they are doing.

and specific feedback is a powerful tool to let teachers know I see—and appreciate—what they are doing.

Although I will always feel I spend too much time in my office and continue to think fondly of my experiences in the classroom, I look forward to spending time with the teachers and the kids here. I can't wait to get my first invitation to lead a lesson.

One-on-One Conversations

Spending lots of time in classrooms and being visible lends itself to opportunities for one-on-one conversations. Depending on the size of the group you will be leading, it may not be appropriate to discuss matters with the whole group right away. You are initially gaining trust, and not everyone wants you to share what you see.

The conversations you share with teachers will be the foundation to every piece of work you will do, and the more time you invest, the more return you'll get from the investment. Make sure to keep these conversations completely between you and the teacher. Building trust hinges on your ability to hear and respond to things you speak about without putting anyone else in the line of fire. If there is even a whiff of a teacher's words getting back to someone else, your relationship with the teacher will likely be compromised. Since this can be damaging beyond repair, be very careful about what you repeat and to whom.

Where you choose to have these conversations matters too; for example, hold non-confidential conversations, especially ones intended to praise a teacher, in a visible location—perhaps while the teacher is on hall duty. Sitting in the hallway, knee to knee with a teacher, is an opportunity to build rapport with the teacher but also create a mental photo op. The visibility will likely gain the curiosity of colleagues, who will poke their heads out of their classrooms, and wonder what you are talking about. Once you are safely out of hearing distance, they will likely ask the teacher what you were up to, and the teacher will have the opportunity to share with them the compliment or encouragement she received from you.

By contrast, however, when members of my team want to chat about new ideas and risk-taking opportunities—something potentially confidential—I hold these in a more private location. While I let the teacher decide where he wants to meet, I make a conscious effort not to pull a power play by insisting we meet in my office, always at least offering another location.

Listen—a *Lot*

Because I'm a doer, listening isn't always a strength, but I practiced it endlessly this year. I recognized early that my ideas weren't as important as those of my group, so I humbled myself and asked my teachers questions and truly listened to their answers. I also practiced *active* listening—not only hearing their words but also observing their body language, tone, and context in order to fully understand what they were saying.

I decided on *attentive* for my #oneword, the word that would be the central theme for this first year, knowing the attention I paid to each member of my team would earn me more respect than would wielding my personal expertise. Not so ironically, my team wasn't interested in talking about my expertise anyway. Frankly, in this new setting, it was irrelevant.

Listening is important and humbling, putting the focus on the speaker instead of on you. Instead of thinking about your response while you listen, fully take in the words and the emotion being shared. You can then respond more effectively from a place of real understanding.

REFLECTIONS FROM A "*WORK IN PROGRESS*"

Choosing #oneword to shape an entire year of learning is always a bit daunting, but I enjoy whittling down my intention to assess success. Plus, the single word seems to magically draw me into focus.

Last year, I chose *clarity*, and I achieved it in many aspects of my life, not just professionally. Taking the opportunity to zero in on what is important and allow the rest to fall away—even when it felt uncomfortable—helped to define last year. This year I need to be intentional about my attention. No longer solely responsible for developing classrooms of learners through one beloved subject, I'm now a team leader, responsible for not only hearing and understanding the needs of others doing the important task of teaching but also helping them move forward.

Taking risks to help students grow has always been a strength of mine. I excelled at building relationships with students to empower them to step up to the high board and take a scary dive for the benefit of personal learning and collective understanding. I've discovered doing the same thing outside of the classroom isn't as different as I had previously thought.

This new role offers a plethora of wonderful opportunities to strengthen my growth mindset while helping others do the same. Miraculously, once I throw myself completely into something new, I'm able to recognize areas continuing to need strengthening. It's like the closer I look (like through a magnifying glass), the more evident those needs are.

I've always been a bit of a loner or rebel, willing to flagrantly break rules and make messes with an end masterpiece in mind. No longer able to maintain this, again I shed the comfort of my own needs and step into the classrooms of others. While these aren't inherently my spaces, I do share the kids. Being attentive to the needs of the students, educators, and others on the administrative team is essential for the betterment of everyone.

So as a new year begins, I again commit to getting into classrooms, intently observing students and teachers interact, listening to teachers share their needs and concerns, and making the best decisions I can make to benefit as many folks as possible. Of course, I won't make everyone happy all the time, but I'm prepared to do what must be done to ensure the forward movement of the team. The needs of students must be the driving impetus for the team's choices and advancement—not the teachers' egos or experiences or mine. This absolute cannot be compromised.

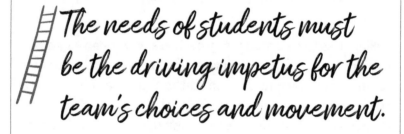

> The needs of students must be the driving impetus for the team's choices and movement.

Knowing that change grows more imminent, I will watch, listen, and respond to the needs of all the members of my team to the best of my ability. Because it will be hard for our team to shift away from comfortable practices, I will need to work diligently to help them shed the old where necessary and emerge stronger together, building our team.

My goal for my team is that each day we will do one more thing to . . .

- Put students in charge of their learning,

- Remove another barrier to the access of experiences,

- Lessen the reins on our control of our spaces,

- Intentionally increase choices and awareness of our own processes,

- Incorporate more reflective practices into our assessment of student learning,

- Challenge our comfort in order to make more inclusive learning spaces,

- Use the right modern tools for learning to better prepare students for life outside our district, and

- Make our team stronger by collaborating and sharing ideas.

New years are exciting. I want to capitalize on the excitement and move forward in sustainable and meaningful ways.

Supporting Your Team Members' Passions

Once you've spent the time listening, observing, and sharing ideas, it is important to support the passions of your team members. Dig deeply to obtain good understanding of what excites them about teaching and then speak to them in their language.

Your job as a leader is not to tell your team what to do; your job is to amplify what they do well and help them want to be better—the same way you did with your students. Learning is personal, and when you take their voice and choice into consideration, you can best honor and respect their expertise and help them develop it further.

This knowledge will be exceedingly helpful in the future also. Taking time to learn your team's passions and engaging with team members about them shows you are genuinely interested and concerned about their happiness. This authentic interest is priceless.

Authentic interest is priceless.

This year I learned there are many intersection points that make it easier to connect with each member of my team. The better I know their passions, the better I can pair team members together and enhance our team in the most amazing ways.

Daily Reflections for Change

☐ How have you created sustainable relationships in your current position?

☐ How have you engaged with people on your team with whom you have had a hard time connecting?

☐ For the good of your team, how can you build bridges to relationships with people who are difficult to be friendly with?

☐ How do you recognize the success of your team members? How do you share the learning with others?

☐ What are your team members' passions? How can you leverage those passions for the benefit of the team?

CHAPTER 5

The Slow-Moving Treadmill of Change

CHANGE IS THE LAW OF LIFE. AND THOSE WHO LOOK ONLY TO THE PAST OR PRESENT ARE CERTAIN TO MISS THE FUTURE.

— President John F. Kennedy

uilding relationships with your team is foundational to being able to introduce future changes; however, relationships alone don't guarantee your team will readily or immediately embrace changes you introduce. Change is never easy. But if you want it to be sustainable and reasonable for the group you are working with, you must know your team and their needs and concerns before heading into uncharted waters of change. Since the level of comfort with change on your team can be diverse, you need to elicit buy-in before you can downshift into real growth.

How can you package change with a pretty bow so your team will more willingly—or even eagerly—be ready to accept it? I have learned the answer lies in when and how you present the needed change. And I can guarantee it won't be at the time or in the way you plan. Because change likely comes initially from the top, as a leader you will know it's coming and can prepare appropriately. No matter how well you think you've frontloaded the expectation to your team, however, someone will always feel caught off guard. How you handle this moment can have a real impact on how the changes move—or *don't* move—forward.

Sticking Your Toe into the Water

Before any change can happen, the majority of your group must be ready for it. You can help them prepare by doing a good job explaining the *why* of the change and explaining its intended impact. You must also do an excellent job selling it to your team members, showing them how it will make their lives easier.

Prior to this, though, you need to get a read on the temperature of your group. How can you do this? Holding informal conversations is a great way to start, but you can also survey them, asking them pointed and anonymous questions. Gathering these data will help you determine the best *when* and *how* to approach the change. You might learn the team needs more information. The more you know as the leader, the better able you will be to provide the needed resources in a variety of ways and ensure the majority of your team members are ready to make the move.

Remember, *not* making a change is always easier than making one. The more due diligence you do ahead of time, the more you will be able to plan for potential pitfalls. Being able to anticipate them also provides you with opportunities to refute them and help move the group forward.

I had a conversation with another leader on our team this year, helping put this in perspective. She was masterful at anticipating what her team was going to complain about and systematically addressed those complaints, making it impossible for the team to say no; for example, if teachers often complained about not having enough time, she planned ahead to give them time during their professional periods so they could collaborate without taking up their personal time. She'd communicate in an email the plan and their options to make it easier.

After watching her in action and seeing how her staff responded, I tried to be more intentional about my choices. Regardless of how excited I may be about something, I need to help the team be as excited, using my knowledge of their personalities, needs, and concerns to effectively disseminate expectations and responsibilities.

As you work toward initiating change . . .

- Survey your team with pointed questions related to current practices and the changes you hope to make.
- Leverage early adopters to help sell the vision.
- Hold one-on-one conversations to identify where the biggest challenges may arise.
- Anticipate possible pitfalls and have strategies and interventions in place to address them ahead of time.
- Communicate expectations effectively.
- Be flexible and learn the needs of your team.
- Be prepared to give up something to get something.
- Know when to cut your losses and start over.

REFLECTIONS FROM A "*WORK IN PROGRESS*"

As a naive new leader, I believed my agenda would be at the forefront of what I accomplished this year; however, I quickly realized my agenda wasn't going to get me anywhere fast. My views were more progressive than my team was ready to deal with, and forcing them to change faster than they were ready to would've been the best way to fail.

Understanding this from my teacher's mindset, I knew I'd need to first understand my team and then determine how best to start implementing new ideas. Developing relationships with my team members and being attentive to their needs allowed me to better understand who they wanted and needed me to be and, more importantly, when I should play each role.

Because leaders will get the outcome they expect, they must make an effort to assume the positive in every situation; for example, adult learners want their leaders to respect their expertise and experience. They want leaders to notice their good work but not make a spectacle. Adult learners want the best for kids. If leaders assume adult learners are teaching because they love kids and want to be the best version of themselves, they will read and respond to situations more positively.

This year I needed to be a listener, a problem solver, and a supporter. I never showed or spoke about my original agenda to my team; instead, I presented information from a variety of viewpoints and opened up group and one-on-one conversations. Ultimately, I allowed the team to select the agenda for next year. Whatever they select will work with the overall goals of the district and will continue to align with the changing state standards for different content areas. Although it is hard at times to divorce my personal philosophies from how I lead, I remember there is a time and place for sharing these. Making a directive isn't the way to bring success.

As conversations bubble up, I carefully play the chess pieces of how to respond, deciding when and how much of my personal thoughts to share. Some teachers can see me as their boss and an individual with important ideas and beliefs. One teacher asked me if I planned to go into state education to assert change in the system. I gave her my standard response to the question: "Yes, when I grow up." At some point, I do believe I will be involved in policy-making around assessment in particular, making it my life's mission to change the way schools assess students. They must move away from standardized tests and move toward portfolio assessment. Students need to be seen for who they are and must be able to demonstrate in a variety of ways what they know and what they can do.

Checklist for Building Rapport

Before you can implement change, you need to know your team. As you work to build relationships with your team members, consider the importance of knowing . . .

- ☐ How each person wants to be spoken to and then speak to them in that way,
- ☐ How each person responds to setbacks so you know how to diffuse situations before they blow up,
- ☐ How to break hard news to folks who don't want to hear it and then support them—with baby steps if need be,
- ☐ When and how to praise each person on your team and which teachers don't want to be publicly celebrated,
- ☐ Who your "go to" teachers are and how to pair them with others, and

☐ Whom you can expect to go above and beyond. In other words, which members of your team are coming in early and staying late? Whom can you text if you need help with something? Who will be willing to do more than what is required—not because they feel they have to but because it is a part of how they work?

Above all, always assume the best of each person on your team. Care about how they feel, and react accordingly. At the same time, however, you also must stay true to yourself and your personal philosophy and mission about education. Although you may not be able to make changes at the pace you want, you should still act with personal integrity so you never lose sight of what you believe.

Walking Back Big Ideas

Sometimes change is like a dance. You present a new idea and then must take a step backward because it doesn't work the way you had hoped or expected it to. Although you may have a timeline in your mind or on your calendar you want to follow, you may decide, especially as a new leader, it is important to walk it back.

At several points this year, I knew I was moving too quickly for my team. Since I was excited, I wanted desperately for them to be on board with me. After one specific department meeting where I introduced many new ideas at once through a jigsaw activity, I realized I was pushing too hard.

After the meeting, I sent out a survey about the learning to get a read on the group and realized many were starting to panic. Based on the responses to the survey, I talked to several team members who I knew would be honest with me. They didn't necessarily disagree with what we were talking about, but they were worried too much was going to change too fast. This was never my intention, but I clearly wasn't effectively communicating expectations.

I had never planned to start changing things this first year, but I wanted to plant seeds for the future. I could have undermined myself by setting the course in an unintended direction. After hearing the feedback of the team members, I clarified my expectations, reminding everyone no major changes were imminent. We would instead work together to determine which changes should happen first and focus our attentions there.

Getting this information was a godsend. Because I learned how people felt early in the process, I could walk back my enthusiasm and move forward more strategically. This way, when it came time to make these changes, there would be a higher likelihood of commitment to the initiative.

Drop Ideas into the Right Hands

As it comes time to make a change, know who your changemakers are and who your team looks to outside of leadership; for example, many teachers in our new humanities department have been in the district and have worked with many different leaders. Other humanities team members look to them for their ideas and are interested in their feelings about things. These folks often have the ears of the people you need to "sell" change to. Build relationships with these folks and then start having one-on-one conversations with them about change, expecting those conversations to spread like wildfire.

Remember, people in schools talk. Make sure you control what they are talking about. Put the kindling into the hands of the folks you know will stoke the biggest fires and then invite more people into the conversation. As these conversations spread, you can begin to control the narrative, something very powerful and important when the hard work of change needs to be done.

Combining Personal Beliefs with the Team's Readiness

As a classroom teacher, I made changes at my own pace—as I was ready. If I wanted to take risks, I engaged my students in a game-like frenzy of choices leading us down the rabbit hole of possibilities. They readily provided honest feedback in a usually gentle way, and together we mixed what needed to happen with what we wanted to happen. I was artful at influencing students to believe that what I was excited about was something they wanted also. From there, we worked magic. The learning orchestrated in those spaces was a continual source of inspiration I was eager to return to each day.

Adults, however, are different. Each has had a lifetime of experiences and expertise dictating what works in their classrooms. So how can you work with them, using what they know and what you know, for the benefit of all students?

In my situation, I didn't know the culture or the students; I only knew what had worked in my classroom where my students shared similar demographics. But my experiences and expertise were very progressive for my new district. I problem-solved differently than I had in past practice. After being in many teachers' classrooms, trying to withhold judgment about what I was seeing, I was better able to share ideas with the teachers who clearly understood the students they were working with.

One of the best ways I found to mix teachers' knowledge with my experience was by waiting for opportunities when they were frustrated with a student or a situation. If they presented a challenge, and I could offer an easy-to-implement and workable remedy, they would more readily trust me with the challenging tasks, such as making bigger changes in their classrooms and philosophies. Soon enough, I would see evidence of what we had discussed in their learning spaces.

REFLECTIONS FROM A "*WORK IN PROGRESS*"

Four other teachers, all committed to putting students in charge of feedback, eagerly participated in the first part of a two-part workshop series outside of my home school. Never afraid to be frank in a realistic way about concerns, they looked for genuine workable strategies for their middle school students. Since all of them were from the same middle school, I had the opportunity to dig deep into their situations and tailor the learning for their particular needs.

To kick off the learning, we watched with intention a great Teaching Channel video I had found about seventh-grade ELA peer conferences. The video generated a good discussion about what we had noticed and what the structure was. Our conversation focused our work and led nicely into a short reading from my book *Peer Feedback in the Classroom* about expert groups: how to create them, what topics should be used, and which students should be placed in them. This led to a bevy of additional questions, prompting me to do additional thinking.

When we met at the first workshop (this was the second part), the teachers had mentioned they previously had a department rubric to structure expectations; however, they weren't using the rubric anymore. After listening to the current conversation, I asked, "How would you feel about working on a collaborative team rubric today and then connecting it back to how you can build expert groups and feedback prompts from it?"

The energy in the room shifted; it was palpable. We already had a professional and collegial relationship, but now the group was excited. Each member eagerly agreed this should be the goal of our session. And while this wasn't what I had originally planned to lead them through, clearly, it was a better idea.

For the rest of the day, we worked through a template the group provided. We looked at each indicator and aligned it with the new Next Generation ELA Standards. We worked through the short "kid-friendly" blurb for the indicator and decided we would write questions for students to ask themselves or each other, questions for student feedback, and prompts for both positive and constructive feedback.

We worked to ensure the rubric would meet the needs of the projects they would use it for. They presupposed the challenges of particular students and worked together to create built-in workarounds. We laughed a lot as we worked our way through the document.

By the end of the day, we had sections kids could use in class for expert groups, aligned with the following standards:

- Organization (for both big picture and small picture)
- Development
- Word choice
- Voice/ Craft/ Audience
- Sentence fluency
- Mechanics
- Process

I'm glad I was able to provide them an authentic opportunity to collaborate and facilitate their work. I'm eager to hear about when they roll it out to students, wondering if this might become a collaborative blog post. As a facilitator, I like nothing more than watching a healthy team work together toward a common goal and then achieving the goal with a product to make their lives easier.

Initially you will find it easier to lead a team you don't work with all the time. Workshop participants elect to be involved in the learning and are therefore generally more open to suggestion and collaboration; otherwise, you may need to take time with your home team, as they didn't necessarily have anything to do with your hiring and may have even opposed it. Patience—and persistence—will get you through their resistance. Be gentle but keep chipping away at their lack of desire for change or learning.

Patience—and persistence—will get you through their resistance.

Daily Reflections for Change

- ☐ How have you assessed the needs of the people in your department?
- ☐ What data have you gathered? How have you used it to impact your choices?
- ☐ Who are the changemakers in your department? How have you leveraged their experiences for future growth?
- ☐ Do your beliefs and agenda align with those of the team? If so, how do you know? If not, how have you adjusted?
- ☐ Where do you need to pull back in order to move forward? How will you proceed?

CHAPTER 6

Be the Leader You Wish You'd Had

A WORD OF ENCOURAGEMENT FROM A TEACHER TO A CHILD CAN CHANGE A LIFE.

A WORD OF ENCOURAGEMENT FROM A SPOUSE CAN SAVE A MARRIAGE.

A WORD OF ENCOURAGEMENT FROM A LEADER CAN INSPIRE A PERSON TO REACH HER POTENTIAL.

—John C. Maxwell

*D*oing what's best for kids has driven my career since it began. In my early days, I didn't fully understand how to "do best," so I focused heavily on my own ideas and experiences and a few texts and other teachers' experiences to help me. As I grew as an educator, though, my concept and skills evolved as I learned to address effectively the needs of all my students.

I often relied on my administrators to provide me with feedback to help me develop my skills; unfortunately, they didn't always know what to say to keep pushing me forward, so I took my first steps toward personal empowerment and teacher leadership and went through the National Board Certification process. This experience was deeply reflective, forced me to analyze my practice in a way my leaders hadn't asked of me, and offered a glimpse at the effective instructional leader I wanted to be for my future team.

Learning and teaching is nuanced. So is leadership. Even with their differences, however, educators are all on the same team—*Team Students*—and they must try to agree on what *doing the best for kids* looks like. I wanted to facilitate this agreement by modeling leadership I wished I'd had as a teacher. I wanted my team to see firsthand not only my view of what was best for kids, but that I was willing to do personally what I was encouraging them to do. My efforts allowed me to continue to build rapport with my team, slowly introduce potential changes, and be with them and their students to demonstrate I was confident in my ability and sincere in my desire to support them.

Ask to Be Invited In

Having a boss come into the classroom unannounced can be nerve wracking and uncomfortable for any teacher. They don't know why the boss is there, and regardless of how well things might be going, self-consciousness and self-doubt bubble to the surface.

Regardless of how you arrived in your leadership position, it will take time for your team to know you are on their side. One way you can communicate this is by asking them to invite you into their classroom when they are doing something they want you to see. This lets them call the shots, but you still get into their room. Allowing them to dictate this part of the narrative is a sure way to build positive relationships.

While asking teachers to do this is easy enough, consider these tips to ensure the entire process all goes smoothly:

- In a department meeting or email, ask your team to invite you into their classrooms. Tell them you want to see the great things they are doing. Point out this is not for an observation; it's simply to give them an opportunity to share.
- After your initial comment, follow up with team members so they know you are really invested.
- When they invite you, be available and show up.
- Before you go to their rooms, ask them what they want or need from you while you're there. Do they want feedback, or do they just want you to see the great things happening? Be clear so you can reinforce they are in control of the visit and you are there to support their needs.
- Participate in any way they ask you to, deferring to them once you enter the room.
- As you leave, thank them for allowing you to visit with the class. Write a note thanking them for having you in.
- If they requested feedback, ask if they want it in writing or if they want to set up an informal meeting to discuss the work.
- Ask them if you can share with other teachers on the team what you saw in their classroom.
- Build on what you saw. Each time you are in a classroom is a chance to grow with the group, so the positive aspects should be developed and shared with the department in a way in which the teacher is comfortable. At first, sharing successes may be hard, depending on the culture of your school. They may not want to look like they are getting special treatment, so you'll need to find a way to help them be confident and also use the experience to develop the group further.

Co-planning and Co-teaching

Co-planning and co-teaching with members of your team is another great way to prove yourself as a new leader, get into classrooms, and show you're willing to do what you're asking your team to do. Similar to asking the team to invite you when *they* were ready, as you introduce a new idea to the group, offer to help them implement it.

When I was a teacher, I always wanted a leader who was knowledgeable about what she was asking of me *and* willing to take the time to show me how to do it. Many of my colleagues shared my feelings, believing it hypocritical for a leader to ask them to do something she wasn't willing to model first.

Be a leader who knows what you are asking your team to do—and why—and then help them see it. Whether you are co-planning with them or co-teaching a new strategy or idea, be ready to show them you know the impact and want to help them be successful. If they aren't ready to co-teach, model the first lesson yourself and then follow up.

In my first year of leading, I was fortunate to get into a lot of classrooms by doing this. All it took was one teacher sharing with others that I showed up, knew my stuff, and the process was easy and enjoyable. Co-planning and co-teaching are great ways for you to write this same positive narrative, and you'll be surprised at how quickly word spreads.

REFLECTIONS FROM A *"WORK IN PROGRESS"*

Today I had another amazing opportunity to co-teach a lesson. The teacher's enthusiasm for having me was exciting enough, but when one of her students thanked me for coming, my heart melted.

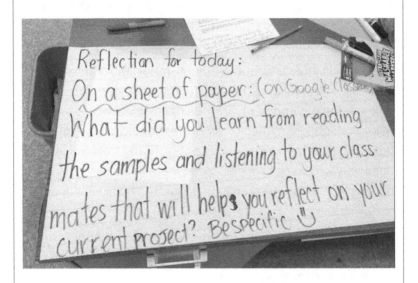

Just because I decide to leave the classroom to take on a different role doesn't mean I can't make opportunities to be in classrooms in capacities beyond observations and evaluations; in fact, these experiences build relationships, demonstrate commitment, and build credibility with the team.

As a teacher, many of my administrators said they would come in to demonstrate new strategies or suggestions, but they never followed up or actually showed up to do so. Some of them didn't even watch me attempt the new idea in order to provide necessary feedback for my improvement. These experiences left a mark on me as an educator, and I promised myself I'd be different as a leader. Today I'm living up to my vow.

Since I started in my new position, I have had the honor to participate in planning and rolling out a project with several different departments—ironically in content areas I'm not licensed to teach (high school and middle school social studies and middle school Spanish); additionally, teachers have invited me in to see the wonderful celebrations of learning happening in their spaces.

This time in the classroom is more important than anything else I do. Interacting with my team and their students, getting to know the environment, and seeing their willingness to take risks and build on their own professionalism and practice builds considerable trust and rapport. Trying new things may not always go smoothly, but I want them to know they have a partner in me; I'm invested in their success because it matters to our students.

Overall, it was a very positive experience, and I'm hoping more teachers will invite me to co-teach with them. I would like to make this a weekly occurrence.

Drop in on Club Meetings

One aspect of teaching I have missed almost more than any has been working with my journalism students. Being a part of the scholastic newspaper programs at my former schools helped me evolve into the educator I've become, so it was natural to want to get involved in my new school's newspaper as well. Plus, I knew I could help without imposing.

After getting the okay from the newspaper advisors, I observed the first meeting and participated in the next. Afterward, I offered to help the advisors provide feedback to the students and offered to co-teach a topic in the journalism class the teacher wasn't familiar with.

One novel thing I did to upgrade the good work they were already doing was start a Blogger account and put their newsletter into a blog format for easier and more effective readership. While the teachers weren't comfortable with the platform at first, I was able to show them how to use it and help them see its potential. Because it was easy to use, they were able to put new articles up as students had them instead of waiting for *all* students to get their work in. This allowed them to get out more timely articles and offered an opportunity for students and teachers to share their work on social networks, increasing readership and building digital citizenship. Throughout the year, we worked together to grow the program, and moving forward, we will offer a more comprehensive elective to prepare students to manage the blog personally.

Like students, teachers need to be empowered to take risks while receiving support as they acquire new skills so they can be successful. This is your most important job as a leader. We need to do this as leaders by allowing our teachers the space to take the risk, get the feedback, and not have any negative consequences attached to the outcome. Teachers need to be able to feel vulnerable around us so they can learn with us. We do that by making ourselves vulnerable and by trying to leave judgment out of our experiences.

Be Where the Kids Are

In order to know the needs of the students you serve, you must be where the kids are. One way, of course, is to be in their classrooms when invited by their teachers, but sometimes you can do this in less formal or traditional ways. One great place to be around kids is in the cafeteria or on the playground, depending on the age of the students you are working with. As a new school leader, I occasionally substituted for district principals and always used this opportunity to spend time with the kids.

When you move into a leadership position, you must be willing to play any role the school needs you to play. You can't be afraid to get your hands dirty. At the same time, you don't want to appear threatening in any way to your team. Consider the following ways to take advantage of different opportunities to be where kids are without making your team uncomfortable:

- Volunteer to help with lunch duties and recess.
- Go on field trips when extra chaperones are needed.
- Visit club meetings.
- Attend sporting events and school activities.
- Visit rehearsals of school plays or concerts before the finished product is ready, then attend the event.
- Be visible during the day in classrooms, hallways, lunch rooms, etc. so the students know who you are and what you do.
- Talk to students when you visit classrooms. Engage them in conversations about their learning—simply because you're genuinely interested.

REFLECTIONS FROM A "*WORK IN PROGRESS*"

Smiles. Laughter. Excitement. Students run up to the school building door, ready for a day of learning and fun. They say goodbye to their parents with hugs and kisses and ascend the steps, smiling at me. "Good morning," I say. "Have a great day." "Good morning," they say back as they walk to their classrooms, ready for another great day.

Sometimes I'm fortunate to play principal for the day in our district's kindergarten center. My favorite "task" is visiting their classrooms, where the energy is contagious. The students' joy is palpable, and their teachers love nurturing their curiosity. Students are always engaged in their learning experiences. As I've spent more time there, the students and teachers have become more familiar with me.

Recently I had the opportunity to participate in a classroom activity. The teacher asked if I wanted to work with one of the students since there was an odd number in the class. "Yes!" I answered eagerly and went to sit with the boy.

"I'm Ashton."

"Hi, Ashton. Can you teach me how to play this game?" I got down on the carpet with him, and he placed the sight-word game sheet on the floor.

"You roll the dice and move your button as many spaces as the number says. Then you have to read the word. And then it's the other person's turn."

"Do you want to go first since you know how to play? You show me how!"

Ashton eagerly rolled the dice and got a high number. He counted out the numbers and then read the word on the sheet.

"I think I know what to do." I rolled the dice, and on we went.

There was a timer on the board, and kids were using all available space in the classroom—some on the floor, others in the nooks and crannies, and others at tables. Soon the timer rang, our game was over, and the teacher called us back to the carpet.

Each child shared who won and eagerly cheered the others on. Ashton told the class I had won, but he was close to winning the second game. "You basically won," I said, "just one away from the finish." He was a great sport, not wanting to lie about winning.

"Thank you for inviting me to play and being such a great teacher," I said to Ashton. As I left, I thanked the teacher for letting me be a part of her class. When I went to her class the next time, Ashton remembered me. He couldn't pronounce my name, but he recognized me and said "Hi" a bunch of times.

Another time, I had the opportunity to facilitate an extra-help group for eighth graders before the state test. Not only did I enjoy working with the seven boys who attended, but I felt even better when I saw them in class or in the halls and knew their names!

I love these opportunities to connect with kids; it's what I miss most about being a teacher. My students were my energy, reminding me every day why I was teaching. In my new role, the students don't see me as a teacher or a role model— yet. But I know this will change in the future as I have more opportunities to be in classrooms and interact with them.

Shifting the Learning Space to Empower Students

As a connected educator, you may think what you do is widespread and common, but this is not always the case. As a new leader, you want to ensure all learning spaces are student friendly. While it may seem silly to mention, long gone are the days of the teacher standing at the front of the room for the whole period.

Telling teachers to use student-centered learning, however, can be scary for some. Reassure them there are many ways to integrate this concept, and it doesn't have to be wild or completely disorderly; for example, you can directly tell teachers they should be engaged with the students where the students are. This means circulating instead of sitting at their desks at the front of the room unless they are conferring with a student or taking attendance for a few moments.

Another easy tip is for teachers to reorganize their furniture for different kinds of lessons, breaking them out of the row mold. Consider these different seating arrangements to engage students in various kinds of activities:

Furniture Arrangement	Types of Activities
Desk pairs or triads	Pair shares or small-group activities
Quads (desks in groups of four)	Jigsaw activities or any small-group work where students need to communicate and collaborate
A horseshoe shape	Debate structures where all students need to see each other
A circle	Group discussions where all students are equal, all should participate equally, and accountability is needed

Daily Reflections for Change

- ☐ How are you currently creating opportunities to be with students?
- ☐ How are you engaging with students to get to know them better?
- ☐ How can you get more involved with students?
- ☐ What does a student-centered learning environment look like in your school?
- ☐ How can you assist teachers to create a more student-centered learning environment?

CHAPTER 7

Planting Seeds for Sustainability

> TO ME, A LEADER IS SOMEONE WHO HOLDS HER- OR
> HIMSELF ACCOUNTABLE FOR FINDING POTENTIAL IN
> PEOPLE AND PROCESSES. AND SO WHAT I THINK
> IS REALLY IMPORTANT IS SUSTAINABILITY.
>
> —Brené Brown

*I*t's not enough for leaders to have great ideas—especially if they can't be sustained. When leaders present what they know to their teams, they must also build structures to help team members develop and grow. Better yet is for a leader to present opportunities where ideas and solutions can grow organically. Ideally, you should have materials ready so when teachers discover what they need, you're ready to provide it.

Over the years, teachers are exposed to many initiatives and strategies. They move readily toward some; they rebel against others. Great leaders help educators discover on their own the changes they need to make—and then smile on the inside, knowing they are working together for the benefit of all kids. I've seen this as an instructional coach this year, helping build the talents of each team as the team's capacity and cohesion has also grown. In turn this will positively impact the school community and student learning.

Lead Like a Talent Coach

All teachers have certain skills that they know they do well and naturally gravitate toward them. But in some situations, other talents are left raw, just beneath the surface, waiting for the right person to notice. As a leader, you are also a talent coach. Your job is to notice what your team members do well—and where their hidden talents lie. You must first recognize them and then help the teachers to recognize and hone them. Building the skills and talents of the team allows you to rely on different members to provide a wealth of opportunities for deeper experiences.

While issuing mandates and writing observations is part of your job, your real work is in the conversations and coaching you do, focusing on teacher growth as much as student growth. You must provide all team members with actionable feedback to ensure they are functioning at their absolute optimal level. Approaching each person with dignity and respect, recognizing what they know, allows you to work together to keep growing as a team.

REFLECTIONS FROM A "*WORK IN PROGRESS*"

I hated grading as a teacher, and I can't say I enjoy it any more as a school leader; in fact, I probably like it less. Since teaching is such a nuanced profession, I find it impossible to authentically evaluate.

And yet, in my new position, I'm forced to do it, and it can put a strain on an essential relationship for growth. Like the teacher-student relationship, the school leader-teacher relationship must seek to promote learning through formative feedback and reflection.

I do like the thoughtful reflection about the lesson that the evaluation process requires. Whether formal or informal, I observe a lesson and engage in a post-observation conversation with the teacher about what transpired. As such, I choose to look at the observation process as an opportunity to help grow talent in my teachers for the benefit of all students. I'm not in the business of making teachers feel bad.

Coaching Teachers through the Evaluation Process

If leaders can see the evaluation process for what it should be—as they did as teachers with their students—they can use this experience to develop strong relationships and trust with their teachers and grow together as a team. As you coach your teachers through the evaluation process, keep the following suggestions in mind:

- Set clear goals in the pre-observation meetings (when you have them), asking the teachers what area they want you to focus on. This allows you to provide feedback in this specific area. Where possible, use the rubric your school uses for evaluation so the teachers can align their practice with the rubric, and you can avoid any surprises.

- Focus on a few important practices and observations. Just as marking up everything imperfect on a student paper will not help the student improve any faster, focusing on too much won't help the teachers develop as fast either; instead, working through a few challenges at a time allows for more pointed feedback and growth. Make sure to prioritize in this way.

- Walk into every observation with an open mind, looking for what the teacher is doing right.

- Shed light on what you see to help further develop those natural or practiced elements already benefiting the students.

- Remind teachers you're a team working for the kids, and since you need to practice and demonstrate a growth mindset, you must look to improve all the time.

- Make sure all elements of the conversation are steeped in evidence, and when discussing areas of need, have a planned strategy to help improve.

- Be supportive to the teachers.

- During the post-observation conversation, again keep an open mind, ask clarifying questions, and fully listen to the teachers. They need to feel heard.
- Be flexible in your understanding of what you saw, but always bring the conversation back to what is best for student learning. No teachers will argue with a student-centered growth model.
- Ask the teachers what they felt was the strength of their lesson and what could have been improved.
- Review data with the teachers and set new goals as you go.
- Be intentional with your words and cautious not to use judgmental comments. Use growth language.
- Start and end learning conversations with positive feedback and stay open to helping teachers improve.
- Ask the teacher for feedback on your observations to make them more useful. Getting focused feedback goes two ways.

My ultimate goal as a school leader is to bring the most positive experience to all students and teachers I work with. I continually ask myself, *Am I a school leader whom I would have wanted to work with as a teacher?*

Plan Professional Learning around Arising Needs

As you get into classrooms and have coaching conversations, obvious trends will arise. Through those conversations and observations, you can begin to build an array of resources and professional learning opportunities to support the needs of your team.

When I do walkthroughs, either alone or with a colleague, I look for something specific from our teaching rubric. After visiting several classrooms, I reflect as I write my thank-you notes, or I reflect with my colleague on what we noticed and areas where we needed to build efficacy. It's important for leaders to be positive when working with teachers and not think any person is intentionally making choices to hurt kids. Assume teachers think they are doing the right thing, and build on this interest.

Make a list of things you notice, then determine priority. Once you know what needs to be addressed first, figure out the best means to address it. Is a private conversation necessary in order to focus on the needs of one teacher or can a meeting be used to share a strategy benefiting everyone? Regardless of what you decide, the *way* you present the feedback and help matters as much as the actual suggestions. Be intentional and transparent, clearly communicating future expectations.

Model Professional Learning

If you decide the best way to share new learning is with the whole group, modeling what you expect is especially effective. Rather than run our monthly department meetings traditionally, I write lesson plans for the agenda. Sometimes spending weeks planning, I decide on a strategy applicable to all the teachers regardless of the content or age group they teach.

Once the strategy is determined, I decide on the content and how it aligns with the teaching rubric to show highly effective practice. Prior to our meeting, I share the agenda with my team via email and ask them for feedback or suggestions of other things they want me to add.

On the day of the meeting, I arrive early with my materials, set up the space, and wait for staff to arrive, greeting them with a smile as they walk in and reminding them where to sit and sign in. I start with my objective for the meeting (a learning target), and as folks settle in, I often offer a warmup or "do now" activity to encourage them to think about how this could apply to their classrooms.

If groups are needed, I intentionally group folks to support the work we are doing; for example, if we are doing vertical articulation, they sit as content area specialists. If we do a regular teaching strategy, I am careful to mix groups by content and age level so folks don't naturally separate by comfort level.

I give directions with a modeled version, and we get to work. The teachers work on the activity, and I circulate while they do. Clipboard in hand, I gather data of what I see and hear, making sure to ask and answer questions as needed. Overall, I make sure to model every aspect of the classroom expectations so they see they can do this if they want to.

After we share out, I email them the exit survey ticket I've saved as a draft on my phone. I learned from experience that sharing the exit ticket early gave folks the chance to answer it before actually doing the learning, which defeated the purpose. While they work on the exit ticket, I remind them I am available to help them try this strategy if they are interested. There is always a question on the exit ticket about additional help as well so they can ask without their peers knowing.

After everyone leaves the meeting, I go to my office and excitedly read their feedback and start planning the next meeting based on what they shared. Sometimes what I read calls for an immediate conversation (as it would with a student too), especially if clarification is necessary. Rather than make assumptions about what I read, I go straight to the source and talk about their feedback. This does two things: (1) The teacher knows I was reading and responding expediently to her concerns and/or ideas, and (2) I am getting more information to better address the needs of a possibly larger challenge. These conversations are less about me and more about listening attentively. With this additional information, I can revisit the challenge and try to see it through the teachers' lenses and make appropriate adjustments.

REFLECTIONS FROM A "*WORK IN PROGRESS*"

As a teacher, I was comfortable making mistakes in front of my students. Okay, not at first, but over time my mistakes made me reflect and created an experience to enrich our learning environment.

As a lead learner, I've learned these "mistake moments" are equally—if not more—important now than they were when I was a teacher. Too often teachers feel like they will get into trouble if they make mistakes.

> Transparency and vulnerabilty are essential to gaining trust. So take the risk we expect our students to take and reflect on the outcome.

I'm learning adult learners are harder to inspire than younger students, but this doesn't stop me from modeling practice that I hope they will take into their classrooms and use in a way making sense to them.

My "agenda" for my last department meeting was a lesson plan. I shared it with my team prior to the meeting as I had done previously in my classes. My students were privy to the actual lesson plan and resources available. They were allowed to question my decisions and push against the plan. I gave my department the same opportunity.

In addition to modeling the lesson plan, I also included a few activities to encourage teachers to reflect on the value of the lesson they observed as well as how they could use it professionally and apply it to benefit their students. I also provided student examples to show where learning could start and how it could grow. Lastly I offered to help team members teach it to their students if they wanted to roll it out.

Over the years, I've often heard my colleagues say administrators don't get into classrooms enough to model the behaviors they expect. Having this in the back of my head, I vowed I would never ask my team to do anything I wouldn't do myself. I therefore offered to take my expertise into their spaces. I miss teaching, so if they take me up on helping them roll it out, it is mutually beneficial. Getting into classrooms helps me develop relationships with the team and the students, and I get to be part of what I love about learning: the conversations, the mess, and the creativity.

At the end of the professional learning, I asked everyone to fill out a digital exit ticket to help me reflect and know where I need to help people. It also helps me get to know folks better. Reading their responses opened up an opportunity for more dialogue even with some seemingly resistant learners.

Despite my own discomfort with confrontation, I made sure to follow up specifically with one teacher, and I think this opened up the possibility of better communication moving forward. I also gained insight into how I might help more of the team connect with each other.

I had assumed incorrectly that all our team knew each other and were comfortable with each other. They aren't, however, so I must do a better job of building the team. Giving my team more icebreaking opportunities in our next meeting will be important to help folks get to know each other better. This is the only way we can then learn better together. At the next meeting, I will also do a better job of intentionally grouping teachers and use this opportunity to help develop more trust and capacity within the team while we work on a content area good for all kids.

I also want to be transparent and share with teachers why I made the choice to transition into leadership. I want them to see my process and not be afraid to shift course if they feel inclined. Transparency was my power as a teacher, and it will be as a leader too. Hopefully it will help the team see me as one of them—not just as the person who evaluates them.

Learning opportunities are too precious to waste. I will keep modeling to make the most of each one, allowing my vulnerability to be visible regardless of how uncomfortable I may feel. My team—and I—will all be better for it later; in fact, some teachers are already curious and are responding favorably to the changes.

Support Teachers in the Way They Need

Sometimes the hardest thing to let go of as a new leader is the way you did things when you were a teacher. Sure, you may have been an expert in the classroom, but your ability doesn't matter if you can't support the folks you're working with in a way that is effective for *them*.

Of course, it is natural to gravitate first to supporting folks the way you appreciate being supported. But this isn't going to work for everyone. Survey your team early to learn how they best like to receive feedback and support and then try to honor them accordingly.

I made a major mistake almost immediately in my new job; in fact, it created my first misunderstanding with the teachers' union! At our first department meeting, I was so excited that it was going better than I had hoped, I eagerly snapped photos and posted them to Twitter, using the school account I had created for the department. While I wasn't doing anything wrong per se, I learned not all teachers like to be celebrated this way. One teacher emailed me directly and asked me to take down the picture she was in. And she wasn't the only one. Another teacher opposed having his image online as well. The fact is, I should have asked first, but I didn't even think of it.

After this, I hung a "no photo" list on my wall so I wouldn't make the same mistake again. These folks liked to have their good job celebrated, but privately or in writing—not for the world to see.

Gather Feedback Constantly

Gathering feedback and data can be done in many ways, and you must try to implement them all; otherwise, you are missing out on valuable opportunities to grow personally and to help your team grow. Since feedback comes in a variety of forms, consider where and when you learn things that can make a positive impact.

Specific Feedback	Possible Use
Personally elicit feedback by asking direct questions—perhaps about your leadership, tone of a meeting, a presentation, classroom demonstration, etc. **General Type:** Formal	Because you asked the question, be ready to implement what you hear. If someone takes the time to offer advice, thoughts, or criticism, you must respond in some way, or you could lose credibility with the person.
Stay tuned for unsolicited feedback you receive in the hallway or other places while you are between appointments and tasks. **General Type:** Informal	While receiving a nugget of information you didn't expect is always good, make sure to investigate further to see where the information leads and how it can be of use to you and your team. Every piece of feedback you receive has its place and can be useful.
Provide a survey to the department or a selected key group, allowing teachers to remain anonymous or choose to add their names. Target feedback to something specific you hope to accomplish. **General Type:** Formal	Thank those who took the time to provide some actionable feedback for the betterment of the group and use this feedback as immediately as possible. When feedback is critical, meet it head on. Own what they are telling you and ask for suggestions or solutions helpful to the whole group.

Be attentive to what you hear through someone else—either about you personally or a happening in the department. **General Type:** Informal	While this may not seem to have a direct impact, it is an opportunity to build a bridge. Depending on the specific nature of the information and whom it concerns, you may either wait until it plays out a little more or get involved before it turns into something negative.
Accept feedback provided by a colleague or supervisor that originated from another source; for example, your supervisor hears you could have handled a situation differently. While you weren't aware the situation was worth fretting over, someone else was. **General Type:** Informal/Formal	Because the information comes from your supervisor or a colleague within the chain of command, you must heed it. Until you are in a culture for a while, things others consider significant may not seem important to you; however, when feedback or advice is offered, especially if unsolicited, this likely means immediate action is required.

Depending on how many people are on your team, the challenges can be exponential. When interpersonal struggles happen with team members, you will need to make a strategic choice about if, when, or how you should intervene. If a team member shares that something is going on and getting out of control, the way you manage the issue with the group will set a precedent. Be decisive and thoughtful but remember to direct your action toward the issue—*not* the people.

Daily Reflections for Change

☐ How can you rebrand the assessment process for educators so it is enjoyable for everyone instead of dreaded?

☐ How do you model what you hope to see teachers do? What is the benefit of modeling?

☐ What kinds of feedback have you been getting? How have you used it to build a better learning environment for all?

☐ Think of a challenging situation you experienced this year. How did you handle it? In retrospect, would you handle it differently? If so, why? What did you learn from this experience?

☐ How can challenging or confrontational situations be avoided or used productively?

CHAPTER 8

Rebranding Confrontation

> WORDS ARE SINGULARLY THE MOST POWERFUL FORCE AVAILABLE TO HUMANITY. WE CAN CHOOSE TO USE THIS FORCE CONSTRUCTIVELY WITH WORDS OF ENCOURAGEMENT, OR DESTRUCTIVELY USING WORDS OF DESPAIR. WORDS HAVE ENERGY AND POWER WITH THE ABILITY TO HELP, TO HEAL, TO HINDER, TO HURT, TO HARM, TO HUMILIATE, AND TO HUMBLE.
>
> –Yehuda Berg

As I mentioned in the previous chapter, interpersonal challenges are likely to arise. Adults, like the students they teach, often experience drama, potentially leading to uncomfortable situations. You can, however, use these situations as an opportunity to build relationships and work together with your team.

Confrontation is never fun, and most folks try to avoid it. I'm no exception. I'm a natural peacemaker who doesn't enjoy conflict of any kind. While conflict can, of course, be productive, it can also be destructive if it isn't handled diplomatically and in a timely fashion.

Politics comes into play here. The very nature of your job is political whether you like it or not. Regardless of whether or not you want to participate, people can be at odds with many of the things they are expected to do—with each other or against the flow of change—and staying neutral isn't always helpful. In order to navigate these situations, stay on top of them and try to head them off before they get blown out of proportion.

Understanding Power Dynamics

At first, I tried adamantly to deny there was a power dynamic at play in my new job. Desperately wanting to be viewed as a part of the team instead of as the boss, I often put myself on the same level as the teachers even though they didn't see me as their equal. This didn't help anyone.

Power dynamics *are* at play when you're a leader. The most important and enduring advice I can offer in this context is don't try to wish them away. Acknowledge them, but don't allow them to control how you interact with the folks on your team. Do the best you can to walk the talk and do what is best for the group, knowing full well any final decisions rest with you. You are the deciding vote—the one the team looks to. This doesn't have to be a scary thing. Honestly, if you embrace the role and seek out advice where appropriate, being the decision maker has its benefits.

As you move into your leadership role, remembering a few key aspects about power dynamics can make your transition easier.

- Your position doesn't define you, but it does put you in a different place.
- Be careful not to share information with the folks on your team that may make them feel uncomfortable.
- Power isn't a bad thing, but you don't need to wield it.
- Just because you're the one with the title doesn't mean you know best. Know who your team experts are and seek their counsel where appropriate.
- Know your teacher leaders and harness their leadership to share the power for the team. There is a lot of hidden capital in the teachers who have shown leadership skills inside of a department or skill, and their interpersonal skills can be leveraged when needed.
- Empower everyone to feel like they matter regardless of who's in charge.

Put Yourself in Others' Shoes

Your being in a new position doesn't change anything about the one you were in before. Teachers are hardworking, caring individuals, and you should never lose sight of your teaching experience; furthermore, your predecessor also had something positive to lend to the position, so don't compare yourself to—or criticize—the way they did the job.

Interpersonal challenges can create conflicts that can easily flare if you choose not to see all sides of the story; in fact, many of the challenging situations you'll face will have something to do with misconceptions or assumptions, adding fuel to the fire. Before making accusations or concluding the worst, go directly to the source to put out fires rather than stoke them. Try to stay impartial by learning all the sides and putting yourself in an empathetic place with each of the folks involved. Regardless of the role you play, each person's part is important and therefore should be respected and heard. Putting yourself in the shoes of those you work with helps facilitate a positive outcome.

REFLECTIONS FROM A "*WORK IN PROGRESS*"

Spring is finally here in New York. While it seems to have arrived suddenly, it has actually been coming for some time, but it hasn't been visible until now. As winter transitions into spring, the barren trees and brown landscape transform into a lush green and flowery landscape. So, too, do the seeds of leadership begin to bloom.

As my first year in leadership draws to a close, I'm fortunate to see some of my efforts flourishing in unexpected ways. While I originally expected to see more—and quicker—growth in my team, I've learned I can't control when things start to take form. The best thing a leader can do is plant seeds and create the right environment for them to grow in.

I began the school year full of ideas and hopes about what I wanted to help my team accomplish. Perhaps selfishly I wanted to find a way to leave my mark, but it became evident early this wasn't my job as a novice leader. My real work was supporting my team so they could better support our students.

I started by tilling the soil: the culture of the school, my team, and our students. I worked feverishly to build relationships and learn the culture and multiple facets of my new job. This "soil" had pre-existed me and would post-date me as well, but I knew it was the lifeline of success, and I wanted to do my part to improve it.

Different members of my team contributed generously to my learning the landscape quicker. Whether in mentoring conversations or early-morning coffee discussions, after asking many questions, I listened eagerly to better understand expectations and personalities.

Next, I needed a working knowledge of the conditions needed for positive growth. I needed to learn the soil's composition, what and how much to plant, and how much "water, sunlight, and fertilizer" would be needed. This came through the process of growing relationships with stakeholders in the community. I participated in school events, attended board meetings, did walkthroughs, and got to know students on field trips and during co-teaching opportunities with my team. When I arrived, I was an unknown entity, so I had to earn the trust of my team and their students. I couldn't just tell them what I could do—or worse—what I wanted to do. I needed to show them my investment.

As months went on, I planted seeds with individual teachers and small teams throughout the district. My vulnerability showed my team I was invested. As hard as it was, I admitted my mistakes and asked for help. I needed and wanted to fix them, and I knew this was the only way I could make myself available to support them in the ways they needed most.

Asking a lot of questions, observing, and trying to stay as non-judgmental as possible, I began to see how I could fit into this team. Gradually I began to share new ideas in our meetings and gather feedback to home in on the temperature of the team. I actively listened and responded in different ways to feedback—both positive and critical. My main objective was to better understand because the more I knew, the better I could approach different challenges. Over time I learned whom I could ask for help in different areas. Various teachers accepted my offers to help them plan projects, co-teach, or provide feedback, but there were still dark days. I sadly focused on what wasn't working.

Suddenly—seemingly overnight—the most amazing things started to happen: People on the team came to me asking about the work they had heard I was doing with other teachers. They were curious and ready to try something new. I also heard about teachers participating in collegial conversations to plan for student-to-student engagement and learning.

Through these conversations, I noticed the subtle impacts I had started to make. Although most of the credit goes to our team members for their willingness to try new things and support each other, I smiled widely, knowing some of my seeds were blooming.

Resist the Urge to Flee from Confrontation

When confrontations arise—and they *will*—resist running away. One of the greatest lessons I learned this year came through a situation I horribly mishandled by wanting to run from confrontation rather than handle it.

Having difficult conversations, particularly related to teacher observations, was not a strength of mine as a new leader. I found it hard to navigate these conversations so that they were both honest and productive. While I didn't like telling someone they needed to change, stewing in possible outcomes only created a bigger disaster. Instead of reacting to the person and the potentially challenging conversation *before* it happened, I should have kept my focus on the issue. I was given this advice many times throughout the year, but I didn't always listen. And when I didn't, the situation went about as badly as it could have gone. In retrospect, I realize if I hadn't psyched myself out before the conversation, I probably would have been more successful.

I learned from this situation that every person wants to be doing the right thing. Unfortunately, educators often believe they are doing their best even when they could be doing better. No matter how senior the teacher, he or she always has room to grow, so approaching difficult conversations without being patronizing can make a positive difference. If I would have listened more, asked more questions, and focused on what could be adjusted—rather than on the evaluation itself—I would have gotten farther.

Just like assessing students is difficult for teachers, the hardest and most dreaded part of being a leader is having to evaluate teacher performance using a system without necessary flexibility for adequate feedback.

With the changes to APPR (New York State's annual teacher-evaluation process) and the expectation of better teacher accountability, leaders must go into each observation process on the side of the teacher, eager to help improve student learning for everyone. Since engaging students in the learning process is a shared goal between the observed teacher and the responsible leader, both must be aware of the purpose of the experience and build upon it.

Unfortunately, similar to what can happen when grades are used for students, evaluations requiring leaders to label teaching with numbers on a rubric can cause the actual learning and feedback to get lost in the observation score. To counter this, as a new school leader, I walk into each observation experience with fresh eyes focused on what good teaching does (and doesn't) look like.

What Good Teaching Looks Like	What Good Teaching Doesn't Look Like
Classrooms are student-centered, with kids doing the heavy lifting of the learning (e.g., students doing a station activity that got them up and moving around the classroom, sharing ideas around a theme related to the novel they are about to read).	Teachers stand at the front of the room for the majority of the period and do most of the work of learning.
Students are grouped in pairs, triads, or quads for easier collaboration.	Students sit in rows and are not engaged with each other.
Teachers are only *one* expert in the room, facilitating conversations and learning and providing continuous opportunities for engagement.	Students work from a textbook or worksheet with no variety and little-to-no engagement.
Teachers use the available resources, including technology, to enrich and enhance student learning.	Students silently comply with expectations without questioning or thinking too much.
Teachers use techniques requiring collaboration for problem solving and critical thinking.	Teachers are responsible for asking the majority of the questions and often answer their own questions when students don't respond quickly enough.

Classrooms are noisy and possibly a little chaotic because kids are involved in learning.	Classrooms are quiet.
Teachers engage students to co-create success criteria.	Success is solely dictated by the teachers.
Teachers involve students in decision making and offer students choices.	Students have no agency in what or how they learn. Teachers make all the decisions for the students.
Students are expected to actively ask questions of the curriculum and of the other students.	Lessons are inflexible and focus more on getting information into the brains of passive students.
Teachers allow for practice time and seek to move each student forward from his or her unique starting point.	Wait time is absent, and all students are expected to complete tasks in a uniform way and in the same amount of time with no flexibility.
Teachers give students the language to talk about learning.	Teachers talk at students, using language the students don't understand or question.
Teachers promote safety and risk-taking by making mistakes expected— not feared.	Mistakes are chastised, and students fear potential— though unintentional— embarrassment by the teacher.
Teachers offer opportunities for reflection and deep metacognitive awareness, which informs future instruction.	Reflection and self-assessment aren't valued and are therefore absent from the learning experience.

Handling a Difficult Confrontation

Each observation is an opportunity to report what you see to the teacher, share evidence, and provide meaningful feedback meant to enhance learning for all students. The post-observation conversation is a chance to share ideas and normalize expectations. But what happens when you meet with a teacher who doesn't agree with your evaluation of his or her lesson despite the evidence provided?

Take a deep breath.

Rather than meet the confrontation head on with additional assertive energy, I choose to listen and write down the teacher's complaints and concerns. This allows me time to digest what I'm hearing and make a determination as to whether or not adjustments can or should be made.

Follow-up conversations are essential once feelings from the original confrontation have settled down. Changes in leadership can make staff uncomfortable, especially if the prior administrator handled things very differently. Your team needs time to get used to your leadership and expectations. As you are developing relationships with your team, they are watching everything you do. Every exchange with them is an opportunity for you to reflect and grow to become a better leader and develop more connected relationships.

As you grow as a leader, patience is necessary. I struggle with this wait time. I expect to be able to do everything right away, which is extremely foolhardy. But I also know I can only move forward as quickly as my staff is willing to go. They must be on board for us to harness what we're doing, continue to tweak it, and work toward the potential for increased student learning.

Daily Reflections for Change

- ☐ What seeds have you planted this year that are finally starting to grow?
- ☐ How do you deal with confrontations as a leader? How have they been excellent learning experiences for everyone?
- ☐ Think about one difficult conversation you had this year. What made it hard? How did you approach it? What did you learn from it? How would you handle it differently next time?
- ☐ What does good teaching look like to you? Is your vision shared by your team? How do you know?
- ☐ How can we better align our expectations with those whom we work with?

CHAPTER 9

Celebrating Your Team

IT'S IMPORTANT TO CELEBRATE YOUR FAILURES
AS MUCH AS YOUR SUCCESSES. IF YOU CELEBRATE
YOUR FAILURES REALLY WELL, AND IF YOU GET TO
THE MOTTO AND SAY, "WOW, I FAILED, I TRIED, I WAS
WRONG, I LEARNED SOMETHING," THEN YOU REALIZE
YOU HAVE NO FEAR, AND WHEN YOUR FEAR GOES
AWAY, YOU CAN MOVE THE WORLD.

–Sebastian Thrun

*S*hifting a culture is hard, but when the team sees you value their hard work and regularly look to share and replicate best practices, magic can happen. Although you may not see this right away, once you do, there is nothing better.

Earlier I mentioned the importance of creating opportunities to praise and/or recognize your team for their progress or good work.

Whether you are visiting celebrations you've been invited to, taking photos of teachers with their consent and sharing them, or having exciting conversations with teachers who have taken risks to increase classroom learning and are sharing what the experiences yielded, teachers are affirmed and encouraged when they are acknowledged.

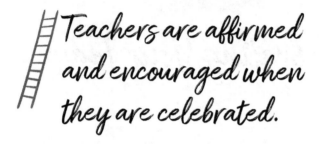

Teachers are affirmed and encouraged when they are celebrated.

Whether you realize it or not, positive things are happening within your team. Knowing about them and participating in them will help make your own dark days brighter; for example, when I had a hard time this year, I knew I was always welcomed to visit one particular class, and I always felt a breath of fresh air when I stopped in. The students were always engaged, and they always excitedly interacted with me when I came by. Plus, since I visited so often, they knew my name and were eager to share their learning with me. Knowing this space existed helped when I needed to be around kids and a teacher who truly loves what she does.

Share Successes on Social Media

Social media is a part of our culture; however, too often the media and non-school individuals control the narrative of schools. As such, it is extremely important for school communities to share the exciting and incredible learning happening there. By controlling the narrative through Twitter posts, blogs, Instagram, and a website, school leaders can ensure there is a balance to what their communities are seeing.

At the start of the school year, I created a departmental Twitter handle (@WHHumanities) I intentionally use when I do walk-throughs or participate in celebrations or assemblies. If a teacher has effectively executed a lesson where students are clearly engaged and learning, I want to capture that moment and share it. If teachers are getting into the learning with their co-teachers, exemplifying the kind of teaching we have been learning about, I want to capture it. The work teachers do needs to be documented and shared; additionally, sharing on social media is a great way to build transparency into the school day.

But the leader can't do this job alone. Build a culture where sharing stories is an expectation among the team and an opportunity for all members to share in the great things happening in their neighbors' classrooms. Plus, being able to see these learning experiences also gives you another entry point into connecting with the students; for example, if a child's work is being celebrated in a different class and I see it, I can approach the child, show interest in the learning, and continue to build rapport. This also works with colleagues. When you get a peek into your colleagues' classrooms, you can engage with them and ask questions potentially leading to future collaborations.

REFLECTIONS FROM A "*WORK IN PROGRESS*"

Desks were grouped in quads. Chart papers were labeled and posted around the room. Clear directions had been both posted and orally presented as well as a clear objective given for why students would be traveling to different areas of the room.

As I walked into an eleventh-grade classroom to watch students engage in collaborative conversations about the American

Dream, I was overwhelmed by the depth of their discussions and ideas about the topics as they approached the theme from different perspectives. In preparation for this lesson and upcoming study of *The Great Gatsby* by F. Scott Fitzgerald, students had been asked to interview a family member about the American Dream to add some depth of understanding and context before exploring the texts. They asked their interviewees the following:

- "What does the American Dream mean to you?"

- "In your opinion, is the American Dream attainable?"

Jeannette Casto, English teacher from West Hempstead High School, asked the students if they thought social class had anything to do with whether a person could attain The American Dream. She had constructed the lesson as a pre-reading, motivating activity where students had to consider the concept of the American Dream and the possible barriers one may encounter when trying to achieve it. She also wanted the students to question if class influenced people's destiny. These questions would be discussed and examined further as students read the novel.

The lesson used six learning stations and did an excellent job of getting students to critically examine and consider various kinds of texts to internalize what the American Dream is in preparation for reading *The Great Gatsby*. Coupled with the carefully planned texts, the lesson also incorporated movement and music to ease transitions between the stations. It was evident the students enjoyed the activity.

At each station, students considered the theme of "class" from a different perspective and showed their group's thinking in a unique color on chart paper. The students, who had done a similar activity related to Poe earlier in the year, knew they weren't supposed to repeat the answers of other groups; however, they could elaborate on or question what was already there.

Station 1: Poem analysis. Students read and annotated "As I Grow Older" by Langston Hughes, doing a text-on-text read looking at five different elements associated with theme, tone, and diction. Directions were placed at the top of the station so students could ensure they were on the right track.

Station 2: Historical Document. Using The Declaration of Independence, students made an interdisciplinary connection as they discussed what America stood for when it claimed her independence. Because eleventh graders in New York also study U.S. History, the students were familiar with the document; however, this opportunity to see it through the lens of "class" added considerable depth to their understanding. Students spent a lot of time considering the statement "All men are created equal" and the implications during this time period when "all men" was not as inclusive as it seemed.

Station 3: Reflection Questions. Students were given four statements they had to read and respond to. They had to strongly agree, agree, disagree, or strongly disagree with each and provide a rationale for their choice. The questions centered around the ideas of "class" and social status.

Station 4: Painting. Students looked at each of the images in Salvador Dali's *The American Dream to* determine what he was trying to say about America.

Station 5: Nonfiction Article. Before class, students were given an article from the *New York Times* and asked to read and annotate it. During this lesson, they discussed any interesting, surprising, or confusing ideas.

Station 6: Creative Writing and Vocabulary. Students drew pictures or wrote poems about the American Dream using their new vocabulary.

Each group spent four minutes at each station, getting through four of them in one lesson. Ms. Casto played jazz music to align with the time period of the novel to help with the transitions between stations and allowed a few extra seconds for groups to finish their thoughts before they moved to the next station.

As the class was ending, she asked the students if they wanted to go to another station or start working on their reflections for the day. They decided to reflect and were given reflection sheets with choices about what they wanted to think about. Each student selected one of the following questions:

A: What is one new or interesting idea you took away from today's lesson?

or

B: Which station do you feel generated the most discussion with your peers? Why?

And each student selected one of these:

C: How would you improve this lesson to make it better for another class?

or

D: Which station do you think was the least thought provoking? How would you change it?

Some of the student thoughts on the lesson included the following:

A: "Langston Hughes not only incorporated racism in his poem but incorporated sounds of New York City which added a new dimension to his poem."

"Racial issues still exist today and play a role in attaining the American Dream."

B: "The station generating the most discussion was the painting because it could be interpreted in many ways."

C: "I would have asked more opinion questions."

D: "The creative station was the least thought provoking because we just looked at how good people's creations were. I would change this by going into depth about the meaning of each of the creations."

"Station 6 was the least thought provoking because it didn't really make you think about the American Dream. It made you think more about the vocabulary. If I changed it, I would've made the focus more about the American Dream and made that the focus."

This elicited a feedback comment from another group which asked, "Can thinking about the vocabulary of the American Dream be thought provoking in any way?"

When I talked to Ms. Casto after the lesson, she felt it had been thought provoking and had accomplished her intended goal. She believed the exit tickets and class discussions during and after each station had helped the students enjoy the activity and achieve success with her intended goals. She also said she would use the students' feedback to further her own instruction.

Ms. Casto offered her students learning experiences, asking them to collaborate, consider multiple texts and genres of text, and think deeply about their learning. I was excited to be invited to attend her lesson and celebrate her as she brought this connected and meaningful learning opportunity to her students.

Highlighting Teacher Work through Peer Activities

Building a culture where teachers have opportunities to visit each other's classes is another way to celebrate teachers' work *and* build the capacity of your team and your school. It's a shame many teachers have taught with colleagues for years but have never seen them actually teach a lesson.

This year we started doing lesson studies, an opportunity for three or four teachers to plan a lesson together, teach it in one of their classrooms, debrief, and then teach it again in a different teacher's classroom. The point is to focus on a particular strategy and see how it impacts student learning. It allows more teachers to collaborate to develop more inclusive, student-centered learning experiences.

Initially, teachers in the same department or same grade level worked together. They were given free time on one day to plan their lessons and given a substitute for the entire next day while they taught their lessons and debriefed. Because we wanted the teachers to own the experience, the administrators were not part of this process. The reflective element of what happened was great for some, as noted in their feedback survey. The teachers enjoyed the opportunity to work with their colleagues according to that same survey.

Intervisitation also allows teachers to learn from each other through visiting each other's classrooms to observe what others are doing to build capacity. If one teacher wants to build their ability to ask questions, and I know another teacher is especially good at fostering student questioning, I may ask the first teacher to visit the second one's room during a class discussion. Both teachers should be amenable to the visit ahead of time, and if the visiting teacher has any questions after the experience, they can debrief. If you have a teacher who does something very well—and you've built a culture reinforcing that teachers are a team of people who can learn from one another—intervisitation can be a great way to share great strategies.

Writing Thank-You Notes

Writing thank-you notes is one lost art that teachers should rediscover. When a teacher or colleague goes out of their way to do something for the team, a handwritten—not emailed—thank-you note shows the depth of my appreciation. After I do a walkthrough, I handwrite a note on our district postcards and share it with the teacher right away. I want my team to know I am aware of—and appreciate—the work they do for our kids.

Unfortunately, teachers—like parents and other people who work tirelessly to make other's lives better—aren't appreciated nearly enough. Make it your job as a school leader to ensure your team feels appreciated and noticed as often as warranted.

REFLECTIONS FROM A "*WORK IN PROGRESS*"

Flowers. Thank-you cards. Hugs and kisses. Homemade presents. While these are all nice gestures from parents and students during Teacher Appreciation Week to show how much they care, one week of appreciation isn't enough. Being a teacher is a complicated and challenging life choice needing respect and recognition on an ongoing basis.

Teachers need to be acknowledged regularly for the time and effort they give to care. The men and women who make this noble job their calling and career path make a commitment to children as if they were their own. This often creates a challenging balance between caring for their "chosen" children and caring for the ones they created.

Teachers often make choices to serve the greater good in quiet ways and don't get recognition; for example, because the school day doesn't provide adequate time to do effectively what teachers need to do, they often spend an enormous amount of personal time making possible the academic lives of their students—answering student emails until the wee hours of the night, reading and assessing student work, or providing feedback to help children grow.

> hey Ms. Sackstein,
> how are you doing
> I miss your lessons
> I think you were the best teacher in Far Rock
> oh yeah I hate to see you leave

The best teachers have systems empowering students to take control of the majority of learning; however, even with these systems, teachers still dedicate their lives to ensuring the success of children—children who often arrive as strangers but leave an indelible mark on them. Teachers teach because it is a part of their soul. Yes, they make mistakes, but they right them as quickly as they realize their error. They model behaviors for learning and take a vested interest in each child. They give to their students, hoping to change them for the better, and in the process, they, too, are changed by their students.

As a former teacher, I understand and deeply appreciate the work our team members do. They come early. They stay late. They ask questions. They care. Every day I do my best to show them I notice, I care, I appreciate them, and I'm here to support them any way I can. Unfortunately, I can never adequately communicate how keenly I understand the amount of work they do, but I can continue to write my short thank-you emails or note cards—and not wait until the calendar tells me to.

Educators are so valued and so important. The job they do is unmatched by any other profession. In the classroom, they are the heroes and lead learners who are charged with inspiring the leaders and innovators of tomorrow.

As I support the teachers on my team to keep doing what they are doing, I will also encourage other leaders to take the time—at least once a day—to notice something special one of their teachers is doing, mention it, and show appreciation in the way the educator likes. Honoring teachers in this way will certainly improve the quality of life in this career.

Students, teachers, administrators, and other school staff should never underestimate the power of a genuine thank-you to sustain educators through darker times and remind them why they chose to give their lives to this profession.

Daily Reflections for Change

☐ What type of teaching/learning opportunities are considered successful enough to be celebrated or highlighted? Who set that standard?

☐ Do you have a ritualized way of sharing or celebrating success with your team? What does it look like? If you don't, what could it look like?

☐ How would you describe the culture of your team?

☐ What was the last celebration you shared with your team? How did it impact the group?

☐ How do you share best practices among the team?

☐ When was the last time you thanked the members of your team? When were you last thanked?

CHAPTER 10

Assessing If You've Made the Right Choice

FOLLOW EFFECTIVE ACTION WITH QUIET REFLECTION. FROM THE QUIET REFLECTION WILL COME EVEN MORE EFFECTIVE ACTION.

–Peter Drucker

*I*t has been a year since I've had a roster of kids to call my own—a year since I've planned a unit and the subsequent lessons for it—a year since I've assessed student work or lost sleep over a student who just isn't getting it. It has also been a year since students have come to have lunch with me—a year since a student gave me a hug of gratitude—a year since "geeking out" about a new idea I wanted to put in the hands of my students to see what they would do with it.

After a year out of the classroom, I'm still questioning whether the decision to leave was the right one. Those core values, deeply set in student learning, haven't changed. Being one step removed from daily interactions in my own classroom has definitely left a wound; however, the wound can be healed. It's simply a matter of replicating what I loved about those interactions in my new position in a way that makes sense for leadership.

Taking on a new role takes time to get used to, and the amount of time needed is different for each new leader. And you may not find a "lucky fit" when you start a new position. You may need to break it in over time with practice and gradually increased comfort level and then reassess whether or not it's for you.

Weighing the Good against What You Miss

If you loved being a teacher, nothing will replace it. But this new position doesn't have to. In fact, use the love you hold in your heart to share your passion with your team. While leaving the classroom needs to be grieved, your loss doesn't mean you made the wrong decision.

Educators need to be lifelong learners, and despite loving what they do, they can easily become complacent when they get good at it. Stretching yourself and considering other possibilities for your talents is necessary for you to be an exemplary model for those you work with. Staying in a position because you've mastered it is good only for so long. Plus, you should leave a situation while you are on the peak and not on the downward slope, limiting future possibilities.

After your first year in leadership, ask yourself . . .

- *How did I grow this year?*
- *Was it what I thought it would be?*
- *How did I surprise myself in the new position?*
- *What did I miss most and did longing for my old position inhibit my ability to put my heart into this new one?*

Sometimes when you hold too tightly to what was in the past, you can rob yourself of what can be in the future. Don't limit yourself in this way.

Expand Your Growth Mindset

Most connected, lifelong learners preach a good sermon about growth mindset and the power of *yet*, but how many actually practice what they preach? If I'm honest about pushing myself and working hard to live by what I suggest others do, I need to challenge myself in inherently difficult ways. Only through this productive struggle can I grow as a learner.

Admitting I was often floundering this year is hard. My pride wants to defend me, acknowledging I did many things well; however, learning doesn't happen in the "well done"; it happens through mistakes. My strength to become a great leader is coming through my ability to recognize, acknowledge, and grow from my mistakes.

Building collaborative relationships with my team and colleagues was a first step toward expanding my growth mindset. It was incumbent upon us as leaders to set goals and monitor our growth against them. Asking for feedback and finding the right ways to fill in the gaps in our skills and knowledge is what will make our district better.

What can you do to ensure you grow your mindset?

Keep yourself honest and reflect regularly on your actions, decisions, and experiences.

Make changes readily if needed.

Read a lot.

Network with other people whose work you admire.

Ask lots of questions and *listen* to the answers—especially when you don't like what you hear. Ask yourself why it makes you uncomfortable. What is underneath your reaction?

Remember that you, too, are a work in progress and may need time to be masterful. Be okay with this. You're on a new journey even though it is a continuation of old one.

REFLECTIONS FROM A *"WORK IN PROGRESS"*

I'm my own worst critic. I often harshly judge myself and expect wildly unrealistic things from myself. I've always been more forgiving of others and more capable of seeing and praising their successes than my own. My self-reflections are critical. After situations occur, I immediately think, *How could I have done better?*

This year, however, I have tried to put things in perspective. Reflection is important, and as I have learned from my own foibles this year, I've discovered writing immediately about my challenges is no longer appropriate. Neither does it mean that I shouldn't think about my role in different situations. I must be reflective to be able to model it.

After sixteen years in the classroom, I got quite good at thinking on my feet, assessing situations, and switching courses if I needed to. Rather than stay the course just to see something through, I abandoned the failed plan and tried to salvage the remaining time. I've found this ability beneficial as a new school leader too. While I don't want to be hard on myself, I also want to balance what I'm doing well with areas where I can improve. As I've continued to practice reflection, I've found several useful things to work on:

- **Asking for help** — I simply don't know everything—especially what I've never been told. I've learned this year I can plan for any number of things, but not for situations and expectations not communicated. Blunders happen because of this, and asking for help before, during, and after situations positively impacts how they turn out. While I used to be afraid to ask for help, now I relish it.

- **Knowing whom to ask is paramount** — Asking for help isn't enough; I need to know the right people to go to in different situations. While this is not always easy, building trust, knowing with whom I can be vulnerable, and learning who will be able to steer me in the right direction is vital.

- **Taking risks** — Sometimes I feel everything I do is a risk as I try to gently disturb the status quo. Knowing how to balance what I would like to present to our team and what I should and can present is always a risk. I need to read the room well and be responsive to what I see. I also must know when to push myself to compel folks to consider something new. I'm not a leader who needs to issue directives to compel compliance; I want authentic buy-in.

- **Getting feedback** — I need to ask for feedback from everyone: How well am I doing? How do you feel about this? What do you think about this idea? And then I need to be open to adjusting my plans based on the feedback I receive; additionally, as I'm assessing situations, I need to see them from a multitude of perspectives. Too often I get mired in my own viewpoint, and this isn't helpful. Getting feedback from my mentor, colleagues, team members, and friends outside the situation is necessary.

- **Continuing my education** — Before I began my graduate classes, I wasn't sure an additional degree was essential for leadership, but what I've learned from my classes I wouldn't have known otherwise. My colleagues challenged my thinking and helped me conceptualize how to do things differently; for example, considering a strategic budget for our department, valuing time and people over things. My law class was also extremely useful and eye-opening, exposing me to specific aspects of the law I must uphold.

- **Keeping an open mind and a growth mindset —** I have an open mind, but I can still be uncomfortable with new ideas sometimes, so I stay eager to keep pushing and to truly listen to those around me before making up my mind. Since I want to do well in this new capacity, I eagerly participate on Twitter, go to conferences, ask questions, and keep learning. My newest obsession is audiobooks, which feed my curiosity and suit the amount of time I have.

Being an educator requires constant reflection. Every choice and action should be transparent, thoughtful, and connected to district-wide goals. Assessing my strengths, focusing my energy, and being attentive to the needs of my team are essential for my continued growth as an educator and leader.

Resetting the Clock

Although you may have spent many years in the classroom, you are new to leadership. Stop comparing your former experiences with what you are doing now. You're still acquiring new knowledge, and you need to be realistic about where you are, where you started, and where you are going.

Admittedly, I feel hypocritical giving this advice since I struggled with this personally and endured challenges all year specifically aligned with letting go. When things didn't go my way, I looked to the classroom, thinking, *I can always go back.* And while I suppose I can, I'm not sure that would be the right move. At this point, I need to look forward, and so do you. If you decide leadership is the right path for you, it's time to recognize "educator" now means something different. Your role has changed, and you need to redefine how you see yourself. In order to do this well, you must let go of "teacher." The good news is you get to reset. And who doesn't love that? You get to determine what this new position is going to be and how it will create learning and other opportunities for you in the future.

It Will Get Easier

Although many obstacles in the classroom were always a challenge for me, certain things got easier with time. This mostly had to do with my confidence level and trusting what I knew about teaching and the kids in my spaces. Now as I look forward to my next steps in leadership, I feel the way Harry felt in *Harry Potter and the Prisoner of Azkaban* when he cast his Petronus to save Sirius: "I knew I could do it this time because I did it before."

You've made it through the early part of leadership, and you're only going up from here. Having a working understanding of the ebbs and flows of the school year, knowing what to expect and when to expect them, and having muscle memory in place will make your day-to-day tasks much easier. Developing deeper interpersonal, trusting relationships is an ongoing responsibility, and learning with your team will grow every year.

But with the development will also come growing pains. I'm still learning about my team, getting more comfortable with when to push and when to ease up as we get to know each other better. While I'm no longer an unknown entity or even new anymore, I'm still trying to earn my keep—just like I did with my students every day as a teacher. Our team deserves the best of me, and I know the more I learn, the more I will grow and push to become even better.

REFLECTIONS FROM A "*WORK IN PROGRESS*"

Perfectionism is a disease not easily overcome, especially when I've spent my whole life aspiring to it and honing my abilities to achieve it. Once I established that there was no happiness—or even reality—in it, I maintained a mindset to keep me focused on the positive instead of my natural need to focus on flaws; however, every once in a while, I still experience an inevitable relapse.

The bottom line is that I expect a lot from myself. Although I never want to let anyone down, I feel disappointing myself is a descending spiral waiting to happen. Thankfully, as an adult, I've gotten better at reframing situations and refocusing on growth. I'm able to look at challenging areas as opportunities for further growth and be excited about them; however, after surveying my team for feedback about my performance this year and advice for next year, I can't help but hyper-focus on the one or two slightly critical pieces of feedback. I keep wondering what I could have done differently and if it would have made a difference.

More importantly, though, the feedback keeps me on my toes. I know what I am capable of, and I'm acutely aware of areas for growth. Learning is key, and starting a new position was an exciting opportunity to increase my learning curve this year. I've learned about creating school budgets and seeing them as a strategic opportunity for growing staff. I've learned about building better uses of time into what we do instead of just looking at numbers. These things seem intuitive and right; I just didn't know they could be done this way. And now that I know, I have a lot more questions to ask. Thankfully, asking questions is not a problem for me!

One disappointment was hearing someone say I acted in a top-down way, when I felt I had done everything in my power to avoid it. As a classroom educator, what I disliked most was someone telling me to do something I didn't think was best for kids. I never wanted to do this to my team, and I'm disappointed in myself if even one person would feel this way. But this causes me to reflect, which gives me an opportunity to reevaluate what I have done, get more input, and approach the teacher to have a conversation. I truly want to do better—now, and every year that follows.

I value the expertise of my team and their input. When I receive positive feedback through an exit ticket after a meeting or from a teacher saying they can recognize my "heart is in the right place" or my "positive attitude and feedback are appreciated," I know I'm doing a lot of things right. I even relish in the greatest dissenters for being comfortable enough to share their differing opinions. To me, this is actually a win-win. I must have done something right if they feel they are being heard—even if we disagree! I always told my classroom students, "I encourage disagreement!" And I do. This is the only way we get better as a group. Of course, criticism is hard to hear sometimes, but it is essential to growth. We must hear where our deficits exist so we can work on them to close the gaps and become more skilled.

I must have done something right if they feel they are being heard—even if we disagree!

As I continue to reflect on my experiences this year, I will look deeply into my learning growth and challenges to set meaningful goals for the future. I will also try not to be too hard on myself when things don't go as hoped the first time. How can I possibly tell students and teachers failure and mistakes are okay if I'm not willing to live by the same tenet? So I'm taking a deep breath and will do better in the future. This is all I can do.

You're Doing Better Than You Think

As I've noted, I find it easier to obsess about what I didn't do right than focus on what I *did* do well; however, while I always feel inadequate when I've tried something new without sufficient efficacy, it doesn't mean I didn't do well.

If you have these same tendencies, try to look at your work through others' eyes. What do they see? What would they tell you? And then take a closer look at your accomplishments. What are you most proud of? How can you build on it for the future? What advice would you give someone else who is where you are? Most likely you will discover, as I did, you're doing much better than you originally thought.

I'm much better at praising other people than applauding myself, but honestly, I'm proud of my first year—struggles, mistakes, and successes. I hope you are too—and I encourage you to give yourself kudos when they're due.

Take Care of Yourself

Regardless of what path you choose as an educator, remember that taking care of yourself is of the utmost importance. Balancing your life with the expectations of the work you do is no small feat, but it must be done, or your career will become a faint flame destined to burn out. You are no good to those you work with or love if you don't intentionally make a choice to take care of your own needs. Honestly, I feel hypocritical giving advice about something I do so poorly, but I know this skill is essential—and it takes practice.

Every day you need to make a conscious effort to eat well, exercise, and make space to take in the new experiences. Much about your new position will overwhelm you, not to mention anything going on outside your job. Keep your priorities aligned so your family doesn't have to compete with your new responsibilities. My husband asked me to leave my phone out of the kitchen when we eat so I won't be tempted to check email or go on Twitter while we are sharing a meal. It's amazing how easily I can get wrapped up in work and let the rest of my life fall away, but the older I get and the happier I am in my personal life, the more I want to enjoy it as much as I want to be successful at my work. Spending time with my growing son and being active outside with my husband make the hard work worthwhile.

As you find your own balance between work life and personal life, consider these ways to take care of yourself:

- Set boundaries between work and home, prioritizing first the one where you are.
- Eat healthy meals and snacks throughout the day no matter how busy you get.
- Find an outlet to help you relax when things get rough.
- Try to take a walk every day to avoid sitting too much.
- Communicate how you feel about things with a trusted person.
- Indulge in something you love once a week.
- Make sure to sleep every night.
- Set up a routine for the evenings and the mornings.

Daily Reflections for Change

- ☐ When you reflect on your first year, what three words describe it? Why?
- ☐ What did you do best this year? How do you know?
- ☐ What could you have done better? How will you improve in the future?
- ☐ How do you feel about leadership now after making the leap? Will you stick with it, or are you happier in the classroom? Why or why not?

Final Thoughts

After wrapping up my first year in leadership and starting over in a new position, I finally feel I'm getting my bearings. So many aspects of great leadership mimic what I loved about being in the classroom. Others represent a new kind of challenge I feel more prepared for as each day progresses.

Folks reminded me many times this year to remember that I hadn't been a confident teacher when I first started. They often asked to me to recall those early struggles before I got too hard on myself with expectations similar to my sixteenth year in the classroom. I was certainly able to get back into my teacher mindset. Honestly, I have a visceral reaction to my first year of teaching. It brought an outpouring of emotions—awesome or terrifying—depending on the day.

But I stuck with it.

In my core, I knew being an educator was absolutely the right profession for me. Ironically, at the time and despite my commitment, I understood what this meant for my future career path. I answered my calling, and the universe has provided me with some incredible life experiences. The students, the learning, my colleagues, and the profoundest sense of awe and certainty all continue to humble me daily.

Now in my leadership position, I must trust that the same possibilities lay uncovered before me, and the adventure will be exploring each of them. I'm excited by how much potential learning I still must do; in fact, the feeling I used to get on my way to school when I thought of an awesome lesson activity—derailing my original plan and sending me enthusiastically back to the drawing board—comes over me again when I think about returning to our team in September.

I'm currently scrolling through the high points of the year and the lessons learned from the low ones. Sure, I've struggled. But I'm far from a quitter, so I'm okay. If leading was easy, everyone would do it, but it isn't for the faint of heart; in fact, colleagues and trusted friends who are leaders have talked with me through many issues, offered their perspectives, and helped me clear the path for my tomorrow. (Now I'm chuckling to myself about how many clichés I was able throw into this paragraph—but nodding at how true each of them is.)

And although I will soon finish my leadership program, my learning never ends. Between the pile of professional books I need to read or listen to, formal and informal conferences I will either present at or participate in, and eventually, the doctoral program I'm sure to enlist in, my ability to model new learning will continue to be a hallmark of who I am as an educator. While there's too much to know and not enough time to excavate, I won't stop trying.

My fears of failure often held me back in the past, but the simple fact is, all my mistakes have propelled me to *now*. And I'm so lucky to be here. There's no easy way to learn hard lessons. If there were, the impact simply would not be significant. So I remind myself it's okay to shed some tears, bruise myself—literally (whether it is my ego or my hips from walking into desks) and figuratively—knowing full well I will heal and be stronger on the other side. And I'm confident you will be too.

Daily Reflections and Reminders

In addition to your daily responsibilities, try some of these tips each day to keep balance between your home live and work life *and* keep stress and anxiety at bay.

SUNDAY

- ☐ Eat a healthy breakfast.
- ☐ Set goals for the week.
- ☐ Plan a calendar for the week and share it with colleagues as appropriate.
- ☐ Get enough sleep so you are prepared for the week.
- ☐ Set personal and professional priorities so clear boundaries are adhered to.
- ☐ Participate in a Twitter chat or two.
- ☐ Do something special with your loved ones or alone.

MONDAY

- ☐ Eat a healthy breakfast.
- ☐ Check your email and calendar for the day and get to work early if possible.
- ☐ Set a maximum of three goals for the day and check them off as you go.
- ☐ Find time to eat during the day and hydrate.
- ☐ Find time to meditate, do personal reading, and/or exercise.
- ☐ Visit classrooms (alone or with a colleague). Write notes to the teachers you visit with feedback about what you saw.
- ☐ Reflect on how the day went.

TUESDAY

- ☐ Eat a healthy breakfast.
- ☐ Check your email and calendar for the day.
- ☐ Plan walkthroughs with a colleague or alone. Write thank-you notes.
- ☐ Eat during the day and hydrate.
- ☐ Make time for exercise—or quiet—to keep focused.
- ☐ Have a walking meeting instead of an office one if you can.
- ☐ Reflect on the day's events.

WEDNESDAY

- ☐ Eat a healthy breakfast.
- ☐ Make sure to eat during the day and hydrate. Try to eat with a colleague today so you aren't so isolated. Try not to talk about work while you eat.
- ☐ Make time for exercise—or quiet—to keep focused.
- ☐ If you can, have a "walking meeting" instead of one in your office.

☐ Review your notes and comments from walkthroughs.

☐ Make a conscious effort to talk to teachers, meeting them in their classrooms or on hall duty—wherever it is convenient for them.

☐ Start planning your next professional learning or meeting.

☐ Reflect on the day's events.

THURSDAY

☐ Eat a healthy breakfast.

☐ Have a conversation with a student or two about what they are learning.

☐ Read something inspiring and share it.

☐ Eat during the day and hydrate.

☐ Make time for exercise—or quiet—to keep focused.

☐ If you can, have a "walking meeting" instead of one in your office.

☐ Reflect and write a blog post.

☐ Participate in a Twitter chat and/or connect with a member of your PLN on Voxer.

FRIDAY

☐ Eat a healthy breakfast.

☐ Check in with colleagues about projects you are working on.

☐ Eat at some point during the day and hydrate.

☐ Make time for exercise—or quiet—to keep focused.

☐ If you can, have a "walking meeting" instead of one in your office.

☐ Follow-up on anything important arising during the week.

☐ Get into bed early.

SATURDAY

☐ Eat a healthy breakfast.

☐ If there are no school activities requiring your presence, take today off. Give yourself permission not to work. Spend time with family or time alone.

☐ Do something for you—get a massage, manicure, or pedicure.

☐ Participate in your favorite Twitter chat.

Acknowledgments

A big shout-out to the folks who read drafts of this book and provided feedback along the way. Feedback is never bad; all of it made my work better.

Thank you to West Hempstead Union Free School District for taking a chance on an untested leader, providing me with the support I needed through a new learning experience, and giving me a home to grow into.

Shout-out to my cohort and professors in the SUNY New Paltz Leadership Program for learning with me, growing me, and sharing ideas. You have all made me a more thoughtful leader who puts the team first. Big thanks to Jill Berkowicz, Katie Zahedi, Jan Hammond, Greg Fredricks, Sue Pariot, Vinny Spadaro, Cathy O'Hara, and Mary Rose Joseph.

A special thanks to Terry Ganley, who is a mentor and friend as I grow in this new position.

More from

DAVE BURGESS
Consulting, Inc.

Since 2012, DBCI has been publishing books that inspire and equip educators to be their best. For more information on our DBCI titles or to purchase bulk orders for your school, district, or book study, visit **DaveBurgessConsulting.com/DBCBooks**.

More from the Like a PIRATE Series

Teach Like a PIRATE by Dave Burgess

Explore Like a Pirate by Michael Matera

Learn Like a Pirate by Paul Solarz

Play Like a Pirate by Quinn Rollins

Run Like a Pirate by Adam Welcome

Lead Like a PIRATE Series

Lead beyond Your Title by Nili Bartley

Lead Like a PIRATE by Shelley Burgess and Beth Houf

Balance Like a Pirate by Jessica Cabeen, Jessica Johnson, and Sarah Johnson

Lead with Culture by Jay Billy

Lead with Literacy by Mandy Ellis

Leadership & School Culture

Culturize by Jimmy Casas

Technology & Tools

Social LEADia by Jennifer Casa-Todd

Teaching Math with Google Apps by Alice Keeler and Diana Herrington

Teaching Methods & Materials

All 4s and 5s by Andrew Sharos

Ditch That Homework by Matt Miller and Alice Keeler

Ditch That Textbook by Matt Miller

Educated by Design by Michael Cohen

The EduProtocol Field Guide by Marlena Hebern and Jon Corippo

Instant Relevance by Denis Sheeran

LAUNCH by John Spencer and A.J. Juliani

Make Learning MAGICAL by Tisha Richmond

Pure Genius by Don Wettrick

Shift This! by Joy Kirr

Spark Learning by Ramsey Musallam

Sparks in the Dark by Travis Crowder and Todd Nesloney

Table Talk Math by John Stevens

The Classroom Chef by John Stevens and Matt Vaudrey

The Wild Card by Hope and Wade King

The Writing on the Classroom Wall by Steve Wyborney

Inspiration, Professional Growth, & Personal Development

The Four O'Clock Faculty by Rich Czyz

Be REAL by Tara Martin

Be the One for Kids by Ryan Sheehy

The EduNinja Mindset by Jennifer Burdis

How Much Water Do We Have? by Pete and Kris Nunweiler

P Is for Pirate by Dave and Shelley Burgess

The Path to Serendipity by Allyson Apsey

Sanctuaries by Dan Tricarico

Shattering the Perfect Teacher Myth by Aaron Hogan

Stories from Webb by Todd Nesloney

Talk to Me by Kim Bearden

The Zen Teacher by Dan Tricarico

Children's Books

Dolphins in Trees by Aaron Polansky

The Princes of Serendip by Allyson Apsey

About the Author

$\mathcal{S}$tarr Sackstein started her teaching career at Far Rockaway High School more than sixteen years ago, eager to make a difference. Quickly learning to connect with students, she was able to recognize the most important part of teaching: building relationships. Fostering relationships with students and peers to encourage community growth and a deeper understanding of personal contribution through reflection, she has continued to elevate her students by putting them at the center of the learning.

Currently, Sackstein is the Director of Humanities (business, English, library, reading, social studies, and world languages) in West Hempstead, New York. While in her first year of leadership, she completed her advanced leadership certification at SUNY New Paltz. Taking what she learned in classes and applying her classroom leadership to a team of teachers, Sackstein was able to start growing as a new school leader, building relationships and demonstrating the kind of leadership she would have liked from her own past administrators.

Prior to her current role, Sackstein was a Teacher Center coordinator and ELA teacher at Long Island City High School in New York. She also spent nine years at World Journalism Preparatory School in Flushing, New York, as a high school English and journalism teacher, where her students ran the multimedia news outlet WJPSnews.com. In 2011, the Dow

Jones News Fund honored Starr as a Special Recognition Advisor, and in 2012, *Education Update* recognized her as an outstanding educator. In her current position, Sackstein has thrown out grades, teaching students that learning isn't about numbers but about the development of skills and the ability to articulate growth.

In 2012, Sackstein tackled National Board Certification in an effort to reflect on her practice and grow as an educational English facilitator. After a year of close examination of her work with students, she achieved the honor. She is also a certified Master Journalism Educator through the Journalism Education Association (JEA). Sackstein also served as the New York State Director to JEA from 2010-2016, helping advisors in New York enhance journalism programs.

She is the author of *Teaching Mythology Exposed: Helping Teachers Create Visionary Classroom Perspective, Blogging for Educators, Teaching Students to Self-Assess: How Do I Help Students Grow as Learners?, The Power of Questioning: Opening Up the World of Student Inquiry, Hacking Assessment: 10 Ways to Go Gradeless in a Traditional Grades School,* and *Hacking Homework: 10 Strategies That Inspire Learning Outside the Classroom* co-written with Connie Hamilton. Most recently, Starr has published *Peer Feedback in the Classroom: Empower Students to be the Experts* with the Association for Supervision and Curriculum Development (ASCD). Sackstein has also contributed to compilation works in 2017 and 2018: *Education Write Now* edited by Jeff Zoul and Joe Mazza and *10 Perspectives on Innovation in Education* with Routledge.

She blogs on *Education Week Teacher* at "Work in Progress," where she discusses all aspects of being a teacher and education reform. She made the Bammy Awards finals for Secondary High School Educator in 2014 and for blogging in 2015. At speaking engagements around the world, Starr speaks about blogging, journalism education, bring your own device, and throwing out grades, which was also highlighted in a recent TEDx Talk entitled "A Recovering Perfectionist's Journey to Give Up Grades." In 2016, she was named one of ASCD's Emerging Leaders.

Balancing a busy career of writing and teaching with being Mom to thirteen-year-old Logan is a challenging adventure. Seeing the world through his eyes reminds her why education needs to change for every child.

Connect with Starr Sackstein:

✉ mssackstein@gmail.com

🐦 twitter.com/MsSackstein

f facebook.com/MsSackstein